MODERN
BRITISH
CIDER

GABE COOK

With original photography by
BILL BRADSHAW

**CAMRA
BOOKS**

For Malaika

Published by the Campaign for Real Ale Ltd.
230 Hatfield Road, St Albans, Hertfordshire AL1 4LW
United Kingdom

www.camra.org.uk/books

ISBN 978-1-85249-371-4

A CIP catalogue record for this book is available from the British Library

Printed and bound in Slovenia by GPS Group

Commissioning Editor: Katie Button, Alan Murphy
Copy Editor: Alan Murphy
Design / Typography: Dale Tomlinson
Cover Design: Jack Pemberton
Illustration: Alex Tillbrook
Sales & Marketing: Toby Langdon

Contents

ACKNOWLEDGEMENTS

Modern British Cider is the result of the actions, support and drive from a great many people. Firstly, a massive thanks to the CAMRA team for helping me bring this book to fruition and for allowing me the freedom to tell the story that needs to be told. Mega thanks to Alan Murphy for taking a punt on me, to Katie Button for keeping me on the straight and narrow and to Dale Tomlinson for making the design process smooth and fun. Massive thanks also to Gill Hough, Alex Metcalfe and Dick Withecombe – CAMRA's fabulous cider champions.

For their help, guidance and fact checking I'd like to thank Andrew Lea, Tom Oliver, Barny Butterfield, Susanna Forbes, Helen Anne Smith, Rachel Hendry, Keith Goverd, Elizabeth Pimblett, Isy Schultz, James McIlwraith, Dr Maria Kennedy, Jamie Hall and Tim Webb.

To my friend, cider photographer supremo and all-round good egg, Bill Bradshaw, thank you for helping me bring the story of *Modern British Cider* to life with your wonderful photography.

The antidote to the challenging process of writing a book during massively challenging times has been The Neutral Cider Hotel podcast. Not only did it provide an opportunity for multiple gratuitous plugs for *Modern British Cider*, but enabled wonderful escapism and sheer, unbridled fun. Much love and thanks to Marytn Goodwin Sharman, Grant Hutchison and Scott Riggs x

To all of the English, Welsh, Scottish and Irish cider makers, I say thank you for conserving our wonderful heritage and for championing our drink to the new generations. Together, we can give cider the respect, appreciation and fervency that it truly deserves.

Finally, and most crucially, to my partner, Jules: I love you and I cannot thank you enough for your strength and support and for allowing me to disappear for several months. This is your book as much as it is mine x

Introduction

People who know me well are aware of certain identifiable traits that I possess - my uncanny knack for being a jammy git, my insistence of always choosing red on the roulette table and my utilisation of utilise over my use of use.

Another known foible is my ability to speak with the aim of eliciting an informed and technical response on a topic, and yet instead undertake a tortuous seven-minute narcissistic monologue that ends in a yes or no question; or maybe no question at all. It's a particular skill.

Well, true to type, I am approaching this book in a similar fashion. I have been presented with a clear, bold and totemic title – 'Modern British Cider'. The natural conclusion to writing such a book, you might imagine, would be to establish, identify and explore exactly what constitutes a modern British cider. Which is precisely what I am **not** going to do. And here's why.

By the time this book is published, I will have I have been formally involved in the cider industry for 16 years, with a few more informal years' worth of 'market research' tacked on before that. This timeframe is (rather neatly) the 21st century to date and has arguably been the time period where cider – indeed, all alcoholic beverages – has undergone multiple, significant changes to the way it is produced, presented, consumed and legislated. And all of this is before we even broach the topic of Covid-19.

It would also be fair to say that, due to multiple factors that we will explore throughout the book, cider has been less quick to respond and capitalise upon these changes. It still remains in a great state of flux, balancing the actions and reactions of established mega-producers, old stalwarts and young upstarts.

So, right now, cider really doesn't need me, a condescendingly moustached Englishman, to apply any form of restrictive definition just as it is beginning to emerge from its chrysalis and turn into the wonderful boozy butterfly that it has the potential to become. Modern British cider isn't a singular thing, it is not a style, it is not a particular process or form of packaging. It can't be a tick-box exercise because the boxes haven't been agreed upon yet. It's more of a free jazz ensemble, exploring all the routes before joining back up together.

I'm talking about modern British cider as a category, a market, an industry, a community, a culture. The world is in a period of huge technological advancement and rapidly altering consuming habits – and then there's Covid-19, of course. This is my attempt to make sense of it all of this and how it interplays with cider; where cider might need to adapt and change, or maybe where its imperative is to stay exactly where it is for the sake of grounding and continuity.

There is no one scale of producer, flavour profile, production technique or mode of consumption that is sacrosanct. I'm interested in cider in its entirety, mostly because I'm nosy, but also because I think everyone can have a part to play – big, small, old, new, rural or urban. The very purpose of this book is to be inclusive, not exclusive.

And so I have spent the first 500 words of this book telling you what I am not going to discuss. So, what is the purpose of *Modern British Cider*, I hear you ask, exasperatedly. It is a reflection of what cider looks like in this modern age, where it has come from and how this informs what trends are being experienced now. It is a look at the challenges and opportunities existing in the present, and into the future, that will influence cider's ability to grow in volume, variety and discovery.

The book is an attempt to disentangle the confused, and often obscure, story of British cider. I am certainly not the first person to

undertake this task. The likes of James Crowden, Fiona Mac, Ted Bruning, Mark Foot, Alan Stone, Roger French, Bill Bradshaw and Pete Brown have produced excellent tomes over the years that describe in great detail the key historical events, personalities and movements. I will endeavour to take this book one step beyond, calling upon these great sources of knowledge and many more to help navigate the murky waters of British cider. To do this, I'm going to need a map.

Cider is embarking on the most intrepid journey, and like any good road trip, the whole experience is considerably more enlightened and enhanced with a map. Consider this book as such. But I don't mean just any old map. I'm talking about a cross between a good old OS Rangefinder and a 15th-century sea faring chart. In fact, it's a map like the classic *mappa mundi* – not just an evocation of place, but of time as well.

The foundation of this book is based upon a clear realisation to me: this is the most exciting time for cider in 400 years. For all the trials and tribulations that will be unearthed, there is a greater diversity of cider styles, flavours and presentations than ever previously recorded. There truly is a cider for everyone.

There are sure to be a lot of exciting things along the way, and also bumps in the road. And what happens when we get to the end of our journey? We'll just have to see. Buckle up and enjoy the ride!

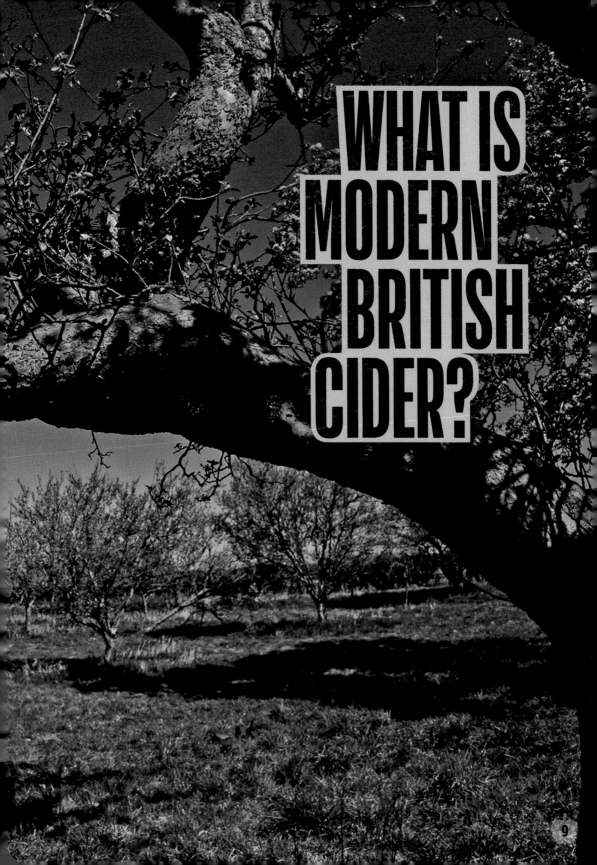

WHAT IS MODERN BRITISH CIDER?

What is Modern?

Modern is more than being shiny

I love researching, investigating and exploring. Inevitably, if one delves deep enough into a topic, one will reach the outer margins of what encompasses the subject matter. Take the word 'modern', for example. Taken to its furthest conclusion, it can be defined as 'space age' or 'state of the art', implying the application of only the latest technology and thinking.

But modern doesn't *have* to mean the most outlandish or the most extreme. It can reflect new changes in technology, trends and habits. Sometimes this relates to the same type of process and production, but with a change in the route to market and marketing.

To be modern is to be current and contemporary – of the now, the present, this instant – but it is not an isolated thing. A snapshot of fashion, architecture, language or computer games today can't be fully informed by solely looking at what is happening now. We have to look at what has come before to understand how, and why, we are where we are.

This is potentially a slippery slope, because, if I was being dramatic (*moi?*), trying to identify significant events that have impacted upon cider could take us back c.3000 years, to the moment that grafting was first mastered by the Mesopotamians. We could even go as far back as 10,000 years ago, when the foothills of the Tien Shan which had provided refugia for *Malus sieversii* during

the last ice age started to be explored by humans at the beginning of their westward migrations, carrying this fruit with them.

As far as this book is concerned, we need to be focusing on the impact of the relevant past upon the present. Given the type, scale and nature of change within cider in Britain, I'm making that call at 1961. Why? You'll find out in the next chapter.

Modern doesn't simply pertain to the process of making cider, of course. A vital component of our decision making as consumers, and as an expression of the ideology of the producers, is the presentation of the cider – the design, the language, the *feeling*.

There are a number of producers heralded today as being on the frontline of modern, contemporary, trailblazing cider who make cider as old school as can be - full juice and wild fermented in an old oak barrel. Now, if that cider were presented in a 330ml can, with clean, fresh branding and consumed by craft beer drinkers, interchanging with their Vermont Session IPA, it lends an entirely different notion to what is modern.

The importance of tradition in a modern world

Sometimes, when it is hard to understand or define a concept, it is simplest to explore or relate to its antonym. In this case, the opposite of modern is traditional.

I suspect that for many people, the term modern British cider brings on a visceral dislike. These people might not know what modern pertains to in this context, but what they do know is that they have a preference towards the comfort and warm glow of all things old fashioned. And with good reason! In the hyper-fast-paced, disconnected, socially isolated world we live in, to turn to and rely on things that have existed for an age, that comfort us and slow things down, provides solace and reassurance that everything is going to be ok.

But when did that ever help society, or cider, to progress, to develop, and to move on? The greatest evolutions in cider were at the forefront of scientific discovery of their respective eras. When John Beale presented a paper to the Royal Society on 10 December 1662 extolling the virtues of placing cider into strengthened glass bottles created by Sir Kenelm Digby and then adding a 'walnut of sugar', this was the first recorded evidence of in-bottle fermentation – and we are mightily glad for it.

Or how about Louis Pasteur and his identification of *Acetobacter aceti* as the cause of vinegar spoilage in wine (and cider)? Even the most ardent of traditional cider makers, foregoing the addition of anything to their cider, knows that minimising air contact from fermentation onwards is key in ensuring that the cider doesn't turn into something best sprinkled over Friday night's fish and chips. Modernity can equate to change and progress with untold benefit to life and cider, even if the cider maker identifies as preferring the traditional approach to things.

Which brings up the conversation of what actually constitutes a tradition? How long does something have to be done before it is considered a tradition? The fact is that cider made in 1921 included some drinks being inoculated with select yeast strains, force carbonated and artificially sweetened. Good old saccharin was patented in 1884 and has been used in West Country farmhouse cider making pretty much ever since. It's fair to say that many people who identify as drinking or making traditional cider might not be fans of these processes.

Why is it important for so many people (in *ciderland* and in general life) to look back, to uphold traditions? I spoke to Dr Maria Kennedy, Instructor of Folklore in the Department of American Studies at Rutgers University. She said:

> The emergence of the industrial era, beginning in the 1700s, begins a process of moving people from work on the land to work in the city, with a loss of pre-industrial farming traditions. Suddenly we have different classes of people mixing in this new

urban sphere – middle classes, working classes, government classes, upper classes, powerful educated classes. They begin to look behind themselves to try and understand who they are, and where they have come from. They see the man in the field singing his song, and they begin to ask what its significance is. This is when the field of folklore is born, as modern people look for the living remnants of a past which might give them a sense of meaning amidst the massive social changes of the present.

By the time we get to the 20th century, everyone is looking behind themselves because we have nearly all moved beyond the field. How can we now make sense of the modern, industrial, and now post-industrial, society that we live in? What are my values? Who am I? The act of looking back and trying to draw upon history is important for our understanding of ourselves.

In order for cider to flourish, it remains crucial to be glancing back, but it also needs to be in the present. This is why the modern age is so exciting. There is the opportunity, and it is emerging, for cider to pull together the traditional and modern, the old methods and the new technologies, the time-old language and the contemporary lexicon. This is the essence of modern and will be this book's guiding light.

What is British?

The West Country and beyond

The development of a true cider industry over the last 500 years was, and is still today, centred in the Three Counties (Gloucestershire, Herefordshire, Worcestershire) and the South-West (Devon and Somerset in particular). The books of the 17th century that document cider for the first time in wonderfully alarming detail talk of these regions as the primary areas of cider apple growing as well as cider production and consumption.

Cider, by virtue of its nature of production, and direct sourcing of raw material, is so much more closely linked to the land than beer. Cider, therefore, is almost exclusively made in rural areas, predominantly those rural areas that have a climate and a long-standing apple-growing industry. And though the majority of these areas are in the West and South-West, there are many other classic apple-growing regions.

The Garden of England itself, Kent, has a recorded history of cider making dating back over 1,000 years, and still has a huge number of orchards growing dessert fruit (though considerably reduced over the last 50 years as a result of the supermarkets' interminable drive for shiny, crisp apples that cannot easily be grown in our temperate climate).

The South-East boasts a proud apple heritage and today there are cider makers throughout Sussex, Essex, Suffolk, Norfolk and

Orchards overlooking the Cromarty Firth, near Inverness

the Home Counties. The counties of the Thames Valley and South Coast span a region where makers are accustomed to using both tannic apples and dessert apples.

And, whisper it quietly, it's actually possible to grow apples north of Oxford. The East Midlands is covered by apple trees in gardens (the original Bramley tree having been planted as a pip in a Nottinghamshire garden by Mary Ann Brailsford in 1809) and remnants of old orchards, as well as newly planted offerings, are prevalent across Northamptonshire and Nottinghamshire especially.

There is an increasingly vibrant cider community north of the M62. Yorkshire has a record of flourishing orchards and vineyards nigh on a thousand years old. Lancashire Estates produced apples of such repute in the Victorian era that there were dozens named after the family of each estate and sold at market.

As we will discover, cider's fate, and its battle for hearts and minds, will be largely played out in urban areas as much as rural spaces. The majority of cider is drunk in cities and increased connectivity to its production is being developed with the emergence of city-based cider makers in London, Manchester and Bristol.

Much of the fruit used in these ciders comes from rural areas, but others use apples and pears from the ever-growing network of urban-based community orchard. These wonderful projects are the beacons of positive action in places that don't always provide these kinds of opportunities for people.

All of these isles

Fear not, my Celtic friends, for I will also be shining a light on producers across the borders – we are talking about *British* cider, after all. The historical evidence of apples being used in day-to-day life in Scotland, Wales and Ireland is about as old as it gets anywhere in Europe, and today, via the magical conduit of DNA testing, the idiosyncrasy of apple and pear varieties from Wales, Scotland and Ireland is known and celebrated.

In Wales this older cider heritage can be seen in Monmouthshire and across the south, with newer, valiant exponents at its western and northern coastal extremities, plus a handful of masochists who wish to see just how far up a mountain apple trees can be grown in the UK before they get whipped into the Irish Sea by an almighty gale or get smothered in snow during harvest.

Scottish cider is undergoing its own small but growing renaissance as a result of the actions of a few enthusiastic individuals. Although more closely associated with the growing of soft fruits, Scottish apple growing and cider making now extends from Dumfries to the Clyde Valley and to East Lothian, with a handful stretching the latitude of growing as far north as Aberdeen and even up into the Highlands.

The Bramley apple heritage of Northern Ireland

Welsh mountain apple trees enjoying winter dormancy

Now, if we're being geopolitically accurate, this is where the coverage should finish. But if we're talking about cider making, consumption and trends across our little collection of islands, then surely we also have to include the Emerald one? Northern Ireland certainly knows how to grow apples, as anyone in Armagh and the surrounding counties will confirm. As far as cider making is concerned, Bramley might still be a mainstay, but now sits alongside a range of fruity, aromatic and bittersweet apples that help create a wonderful range of different styles. And although the Republic has to deal with a host of different factors, it still does the trick of growing great apples and making great cider, especially in the Cork, Tipperary and Meath areas.

It would have been impossible for me to cover such ground ten, or maybe even five, years ago. To be able to include makers from all corners of Britain is testament, once again, to cider's tangible rise.

What is Cider?

Many things to many people

From a cider making perspective, the answer to this question should be pretty cut and dried: cider is an alcoholic beverage derived from the fermentation of apple juice.

Boom. Job done. Move on. Well, as we're starting to discover, when it comes to cider, things are never that simple. We're going to need to dig a little deeper.

For many makers and passionate fans of cider, in Britain and beyond, the above description is precisely what cider is, should be and could only ever be – the juice, the whole juice and nothing but the juice, with nothing added and nothing taken away.

For the average consumer, however, the perception of cid er is largely driven by formative drinking experiences of ciders that diverge from this idyllic interpretation, frequently with a negative outcome. The same stories about cider are constantly reiterated: illicit drinking from plastic bottles on the park bench, being violently ill at the house party after 19 cans of 'Sledgehammer', it being too strong or too sweet.

How has that situation arisen? Well, much like any other item of food and drink with historic roots, there has been continued development of processing and stabilising techniques that have enabled them to become more widely, and easily, consumable products.

As with most aspects of our everyday lives, however, there are interpretations of a subject matter by individuals and groups, and then there is definition by law. We'll have plenty of time to delve into consumer insight as we examine this further, so it's probably wise to have a look at the law at this point.

HMRC Notice 162

The primary piece of legislation that defines beers, wines, spirits and ciders comes in the form of the Alcoholic Liquor Duties Act (ALDA) 1979. This is, in fact, the only piece of legislation that exists for cider. Continuing the tricky theme of wrangling with British cider, the definition is quite convoluted and lengthy. The definitions for spirits, wine and beer amount to 60, 45 and 40 words respectively – for cider, it tops a whopping 315 words.

In fact, it is so tricky it has to be split into four sections:

a)   cider or perry of a strength exceeding 1.2% alcohol by volume (ABV) but less than 8.5% ABV;

b)   obtained from the fermentation of apple or pear juice without the addition at any time of any alcoholic liquor or of any liquor or substance which communicates colour or flavour other than such as the Commissioners may allow as appearing to them to be necessary to make cider or perry;

c)   the pre-fermentation mixture for which satisfies the pre-fermentation juice requirement;

d)   which satisfies the final product juice requirement.

(As an aside, who are these mysterious commissioners? The Druids? Men in dark suits at the Pentagon smoking endless cigarettes in the shadows? Or just a junior civil servant from Croydon? I wonder...)

On the face of it, sections a) and b) are actually pretty similar to the *Dummies Guide to ...* definition at the beginning of this section. Except for the fact that there are actually quite a few things that the commissioners allow as being necessary to make cider or perry.

Without wishing to delve too deeply into the convoluted world of UK legislation, these regulations are managed under a section of HMRC called Notice 162 (you might hear people reference this from time to time, with a painful, distant look in the eye). That's right – in practice, this definition is only administered for tax purposes.

So just what is permitted? These include things that are maybe not unexpected and are understood as being part of a modern cider making system that helps ensure products are presented to consumers in an appealing and presentable fashion, such as sugar, carbon dioxide and sulphur dioxide.

But it also includes some items that feel, to me anyhow, a little archaic today, but were certainly reflective of the level of food standards in the UK in 1976:

- Artificial sweeteners sweets such as Acelsufame K, Neohesperidine, and good old Saccharin

- Artificial colours such as acid brill green E142, sunset yellow E110 and tartrazine E102

As it happens, the permitted ingredient that causes the greatest level of disagreement amongst cider makers is pure, natural and something that is essential to human life. I'm talking about **water**.

The addition of water to pre-formented juice and to fermented cider has happened, and will continue to happen, for an age. Rewetting pomace, flavour amelioration, alcohol percentage adjustment and dissolving of processing aids all require the use of water – nothing too outlandish there (although many purists will give me a quick shin kick for spouting such tosh). No, the major fallout comes with the use of water for the primary purpose of 'value engineering' – maximising volume while minimising the raw material content (i.e., apple juice).

Sections c) and d) of ALDA 1979 (listed above) pertain to this hottest of cider-flavoured potatoes. Here's the plain-speak version:

c) cider makers must ensure that the juice they have prior to fermentation is at least as juicy as a really unripe apple (i.e., you're able to dilute your juice with a bit of water to a certain point and it still be considered 100% juice).

d) once you have your fermented 'base cider' (which could have been achieved with the addition of a load of extra sugar into the juice so that the alcohol could be sitting around 14% ABV) it can be further diluted with water to a minimum of 35% equivalent juice.

What is even more troubling is that this 35% figure can also include juice added post-fermentation for sweetening purposes. So, it would be the case that a cider could have a c.30% fermented juice content, with the extra 5% being unfermented and added just prior to packaging.

The '35% Minimum Juice' issue is a complex, technical beast and, understandably, it is a massive bone of contention for many producers and campaigners. In fact, it is often seen as the key factor that divides the cider category. Although, as you will discover, I am not an advocate of ciders that aim for the lowest possible juice content, I will be exploring, and even endorsing, those that are **not** 100% juice. I do this because I fundamentally do not believe that 100% juice cider is automatically 'better' than a cider with the addition of some water. There are far too many other parameters, considerations and interpretations that can come into play, and which can be subjective, sensorial or ideological.

Flavoured ciders

The second grenade that ALDA 1979 lobs in our direction is the omission on the permitted ingredients list of any fruit (other than apple/pear), any vegetables, herbs, spices, honey, etc. What this means to say is that, in the eyes of the tax officials, the controversial category of Flavoured Ciders is not cider at all. This fact gives the cider purists much cause for wailing and gnashing of teeth and protestation. How can these products be considered cider, and allowed to be called cider, if they can't be taxed as cider? The answer is that taxation and labelling are entirely different concepts, governed by entirely different regulations.

So how is the word cider defined on a label? For this we must look at the Food Labelling Regulations (1996). Ultimately, if no pre-existing term exists for a consumable food or drink (let's say blackberry cider), then the producer is encouraged to make the description obvious enough for the layman on the street to understand – i.e., use common sense!

So there you have it. Although not covered by the definition in law, blackberry cider could be fairly considered to describe the true nature of the food, and certainly today, with the proliferation of flavoured ciders, would be considered a customary term.

If blackberry cider and its friends aren't governed by HMRC Notice 162, then where does this take place? Well, the answer is the confusingly similarly named HMRC Notice 163, which covers wine, and, in the case of blackberry cider, 'Made Wine'. Again, this is a term you might hear bandied around, often followed by a derisory spit of chewing tobacco onto the floor (if we were suddenly transported to Gold Rush era California).

Brace yourself, but I will be including blackberry cider, indeed, all flavoured ciders, within the pages of this book. Why? Because this is a book for everyone who makes, sells and drinks cider, not a myopic and dogmatic treatise from someone only passionate about a particular style of cider. Consumers consider these drinks to be a type of cider, pubs consider these drinks to be a type of cider, and an increasing number of producers at the smaller, even traditional, end of the spectrum consider these drinks to be a type of cider.

Some object to flavoured ciders, arguing that 'cider doesn't need anything added to it'. Of course, you don't *need* to add elderflowers to a cider in order for it to be a superior product. Neither do you *need* to add wheat or raspberries to a beer to make it 'better' – but you can, and this has been done for a little while. I am an advocate of playfulness, experimentation and reaching new drinkers – important actions in a modern world – and flavoured ciders, if made with skill, care and respect, have the opportunity to do this.

Fret ye not if you don't like the sound of this, however, for I will be going on to explore the nature of flavoured cider in its entirety and conclude that many of the flavoured brands in the marketplace do not deserve (in my opinion) to bear the name cider. It comes down to a simple maxim for me: I'm not anti-flavoured cider, but I am opposed to flavoured, indeed any, cider, that is so far removed from fermented apple character that the alcohol could be derived from any source. Alas, many of the top flavoured cider brands available in Britain today, originating from these shores or otherwise, are execrable and not much more than sugar-laden, artificially flavoured, alcopops-by-proxy.

Perry

And finally, before any '*Pyrus* Maniacs' (see what I did there?) start kicking off, it goes without saying that the product of fermented pear juice will be included in this tome. Being born into the Perry Motherland, but a few miles from May Hill in Gloucestershire, its spiritual epicentre in Britain, perry is something I care for deeply. I wish to ensure that the culture and heritage of this mystical drink, and of those majestic trees that bear the fruits of its production, are retained for generations to come.

So, we can assume that when I am talking about cider, I will be talking about perry, too. It's just that not adding the words 'and perry' after every time I mention the word cider is going to save my keyboard some considerable wear and tear.

So, there you have it. We're going to be exploring a whole raft of differing ciders: from those with 35% juice to 100% juice; maturing for two weeks or two years; made in old wooden vessels or shiny steel tanks; flavoured with Damson to only flavoured with Dabinett. If you've made it this far and you're still willing to continue on the journey with me, take a good hold of the map and hold on tight because, although this the most exciting time for cider, it's also possibly the most tumultuous. Are you ready? Ok, let's go!

THE SHAPING OF MODERN BRITISH CIDER

Ten Key Events

1961 – Acquisition of Taunton Cider by the brewers

Out the gloom of the initial post-war era, especially once rationing ended, came a boom in consumer spending. A higher disposable income, technological advancements and a bold, entrepreneurial drive from producers of all consumable items, including food and drink, ensured that new products and new trends emerged at a rapid pace.

The brewers of Britain burst into the 1950s with an attitude of wanting to satisfy this new desire for consumption. They sought to achieve quick growth, servicing a national marketplace. This was most easily undertaken through the acquisition of smaller brewers for the purpose of gaining control of their pub estate, their key brands and to reduce the of number of competing brands in the market. The number of regional, independent brewers and brewpubs diminished rapidly, hastening a trend that would last for the rest of the 20th century. An increasingly smaller number of larger breweries controlled the beer market.

Cider, being the rurally produced and land-tied beverage that it was (and essentially still is), ensured that the number of commercial cider makers, and the access to the national marketplace, was always going to be playing second fiddle to beer. Only a handful of cider makers emerged through the 20th century with the desire and business clout to become national cider makers and sit alongside the big brewers.

HP Bulmer Ltd (Bulmers) was one such cider maker. Established in 1887 by H. P. (Percy) Bulmer, and joined a year later by his brother E. F. (Fred) Bulmer, they revolutionised British cider forever, establishing a commercial enterprise model for cider making. Post 1945, Bulmers, with a keen eye upon the successful activities of the bigger brewers, undertook their own set of acquisitions to consolidate their position as Britain's biggest producer, and to retain control of route to market through the pub deals these smaller cider makers had established. This takes in Godwin's of Herefordshire (1948), Gloucestershire Cider Co at Wickwar (1959), William Evans of Herefordshire (1960) and Tewkesbury Cider Co (1965).

But Bulmers wasn't the only major player. Showerings of Shepton Mallett, Somerset, were also making a play for South-West regional, and indeed national domination. Much like Bulmers, they followed the aggressive path of the brewers, purchasing Coates of Nailsea, Somerset (1956), before subsequently merging with Whiteways of Devon (1959) and Gaymers of Attleborough, Norfolk (1961), creating a nationally powerful cider (and perry) making enterprise.

But the most significant step was to come. Thanks to the expansion of these larger cider makers, and their entrenched relationship with breweries, cider was becoming a mainstay in pubs across the country. Several brewers came to the same conclusion, that they could save money on ciders being sold in their pubs if they actually owned the cider maker. Enter The Taunton Cider Co. Established in 1911 in Norton Fitzwarren and having secured strong volume growth in the 1950s through quality control improvements and swallowing up some smaller Somerset makers, they were purchased by a consortium of breweries in 1961, largely at the instigation of Courage. They were later joined by Bass and others before Guinness joined in 1971 to cement its major player status in British cider making.

This milestone marked Big Beer's first involvement with cider and precipitated some significant developments that are still being felt today. It choked the supply of cider into pubs, with the primary route to market for smaller regional cider makers removed. With just one line being dedicated to it, cider was never afforded the opportunity to showcase the range of different flavours and styles it can possess. Beer was able to demonstrate Lager, Stout, Mild, Bitter and IPA. Cider was able to demonstrate... well, just cider. Being viewed as a singular style and being given only one opportunity to demonstrate that style per pub is predominantly where cider still exists today, with the majority of nuance coming solely in the level of sweetness or alcoholic strength, or addition of flavours.

Secondly, this 'beerification' of cider (allied to a challenging duty system from 1976) facilitated the end of commercially viable, independent, regional mid-scale cider makers. In today's market, to survive as a cider maker you have to be huge (with economies of scale to satisfy the micro-margins being achieved across a vast volume) or approach from a low-volume/high-value position.

*

The 'beerification' of cider from the 1960s didn't solely extend to its route to market. It ushered in an era of 'shaking things up' and aggressively introducing brewing practices at all levels, with the intent of making cider more cheaply and consistently. This ideology led to the adoption by the biggest cider makers of two key practices: making cider from apple juice concentrate (AJC), and the chaptalisation (see below) of juice.

The purchasing of AJC, rather than fresh apples, for turning into cider had been undertaken before the Second World War to help plug any gaps in the supply of raw material as a result of a bad harvest. AJC, however, was expensive at this point, and it was only from the 1960s that purchasing AJC from the global spot market and/or converting British apples into concentrate became more commonplace.

When a cider maker reaches a certain scale, the shift from classic 'harvest/ferment/mature/draw down as needed' to 'produce on demand' is increasingly attractive:

- considerably less tank space is needed;

- greater levels of flavour profile consistency can be achieved;

- easily achieves clean/easy flavour profile with little maturation time;

- if purchasing dessert AJC from Europe, Asia or South America, this will be the cheapest source of juice that can be made into cider.

The making of cider from AJC today accounts for the vast majority of cider volumes all across the globe. These are liquids that do not endeavour to do anything other than convey a fresh, clean, long alcoholic drink experience, which, as anyone who has tasted a foul, acetic-riddled cider will confirm, is no bad thing.

It's important to assess the nature of the AJC before passing too much comment on it. A large chunk of the opprobrium directed towards AJC is on account of much of it being non-British in origin,

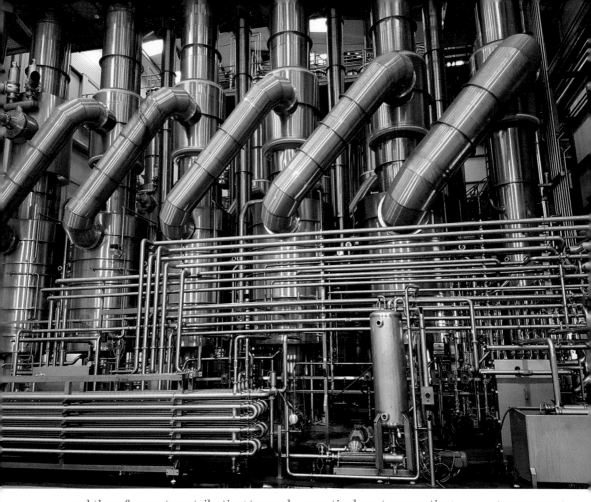

and therefore not contributing towards, or actively out-competing, British agriculture. The harrowing sight of orchards being pulled out of the ground in the shires while cider volumes show (in non-Covid times) slight growth is testament to this (to be discussed further in the next chapter). However, the majority of AJC used in British cider *is* made from British apples, typically grown by the makers themselves and under contract to local farmers. The fact that the resultant juice is concentrated does nothing to diminish the positive impact that the orchards bring to communities, to landscape and to biodiversity, as well as providing a significant contribution to the rural economies of the growing regions.

Is the use of AJC the work of the devil? No. Is AJC the ultimate arbiter of a 'bad' cider? No. Can the use of AJC equate to ciders of mystique, excitement, flavour intensity, elegance or finesse? No.

An evaporator for creating apple juice concentrate

However, I can't help but feel that using AJC instead of fresh apple juice not only loses all sense of flavour and aroma intensity and complexity, but, more crucially, serves to dumb down the magic and wonder of what cider is. It certainly serves to facilitate the commodification and lack of reverence of cider amongst a significant proportion of the population.

Fundamentally, I believe in the opportunity for the consumer to make their own decision on which cider to purchase, made from AJC or otherwise, but I wish for them to be fully informed in their decision making, which currently is not the norm given the paucity of ingredients listed by the vast majority of cider brands.

✳

The second value-engineering tool ushered in with the brewing mindset was a process called chaptalisation. Developed by a Monsieur Chaptal in France in 1801, originally as a method of improving preservation of wines, chaptalisation is the process of adding sugar to unfermented grape or apple juice in order to increase alcohol content after fermentation. Today, where permitted, chaptalisation in wine takes place in years when insufficient natural sugars have built up in grapes, as a result of poor weather, to create the requisite level of alcohol to satisfy the flavour and structure demands of the specific style.

The use of chaptalisation in cider was not something the brewers invented. State regulations in France in 1933 explicitly permitted 'the sweetening of apple juice by the unlimited quantities of sucrose provided it does not alter the essential nature of the product.' In Britain, the National Mark scheme to designate the best of British Cider – *Select Cider or Select Cyder* – also permitted the addition of sugar syrup prior to fermentation as far back as 1931.

The common use of chaptalisation began once post-war sugar rationing ended in the 1960s, and as the practice of adjuncts transcended from brewing to cider making, the use of glucose syrups began to be widely adopted by cider makers from the 1970s.

Unlike wine's original and continued (where regionally permitted) use of chaptalisation to aid preservation and style, in the world of cider, chaptalisation is primarily, and entirely legally, used by the larger makers to achieve a high alcohol base cider – somewhere in the 10–14% ABV region. Prior to packaging, this base cider is then diluted with water to reach the target alcohol level, normally between 4 and 8.4% ABV, sometimes resulting in the final product containing a minority of fermented apple base and a majority of water. Why do this? Bluntly, to maximise volume of final product that can be achieved in a cheap fashion – water and sugar being cheaper than apple juice.

I want to make clear that chaptalisation is not a dirty word. As ever, it's a matter of context, nuance and motivation. To lightly chaptalise juice such that it can guarantee the consistent ABV and flavour intensity of a suite of brands, or to significantly chaptalise in the endeavour of creating an apple wine (possibly fully bottle-fermented and oozing elegance and class), are simply a part of the cider maker's armoury.

As will become apparent, I do not hold the highest possible juice content as the ultimate arbiter of cider quality, but surely the best of cider cannot be achieved with intense chaptalisation and dilution? When a cider on the shelf contains more water than fermented base cider, then, fundamentally, something isn't right.

1962 – Strongbow launches in keg

This period not only saw advancement in the modernising of liquid production and packaging, but also the presentation. The power of marketing and advertising surged in the 1950s (as any devotee of *Mad Men* will attest to) as brands wished to appeal to these newly upwardly mobile consumers with discretionary spending opportunities. The power of *brand* came to the fore and cider was no different.

This is not to say that prior to the 1950s no cider brands existed – far from it. Woodpecker, from Bulmers, was launched in 1894

and remains the world's oldest cider brand, while Showerings'
Babycham can lay claim to being the first alcoholic drink of
any kind to be advertised on TV in 1957.

The key brand that ushered in the modern marketing
mindset, however, was Strongbow from Bulmers. From top to tail,
Strongbow is a masterclass in brand development. First launched
in 1960 in bottle, it was explicitly developed as a brand to compete
with, and appeal to, the increasing numbers of drinkers of fizzy
beer – specifically Lager. Aimed at 18–24 year-olds with greater
disposable income and a zest for life, the biggest step came with
Strongbow's availability in keg for the first time in 1962.

These drinkers were, of course, mostly men, and a strong drive
for masculinity was front and centre in Strongbow's marketing.
Can you get a more masculine brand than one which emphasises
strength through the explicit use of the word 'strong' in the brand
name, and that features the icon of a warrior? There's no beating
about the bush here.

Early TV advertising featured a young George Lazenby (pre-
Bond), chiselled of jaw and furrowed of brow, walking across the
hills in a nice woollen jersey armed with a handle of Strongbow.
But soon the attention of the marketing directors turned to being
playful through the concepts of strength, masculinity, and crucially,
given the drive for drinking by the pint, the allure of the pub culture.
The straplines of the key adverts from those decades gives some
indication of the intention of the brand:

> 1960s – 'A new drink that fixes a man-sized thirst';
> 1973 – 'Strong as your thirst';
> 1986 – 'Strong, Straight, True';
> 1990s – 'Live to Loaf' (the smarmy laddishness of the 90s
> personified through Johnny Vaughan).

Amongst the cringe-inducing Strongbow adverts were the odd
gem, spawning the efforts of numerous other brands to compete.
Dry Blackthorn produced a series of 'down the pub' adverts directly

aimed at the male pub drinker, but most amazingly were the series of budget-busting TV adverts featuring Leslie Nielsen, right in the middle of his *Police Squad* fame. The advertised cider was a now non-existent brand from Taunton Cider called Red Rock (have a Google search – it's quite amazing).

Strongbow marketing at the peak of 1990s laddish culture

✳

So how is the impact of Strongbow's 60-year drive to compete with Lager still impacting cider today? Well, firstly, it is far and away the world's largest cider brand. It has certainly achieved its intention of being a competitor to Lager, with both the 'Original' and more recent 'Dark Fruits' variation featuring in the top 10 best-selling pints. Combine the volumes of the two variations together and Strongbow would sit in third place behind Carling and Fosters.

Prior to the advent of the 'Magner's Effect' and flavoured ciders, cider in Britain (at odds with virtually every other global market) was viewed as a masculine drink, largely down to the considerable efforts of the Strongbow brand team.

Most crucially, Strongbow has engendered the concept of mainstream cider – aka 'cider as Lager' – as a long drink of around 4.5%–5% ABV, with sufficient sweetness, acidity and chill factor to be consumed sessionably by the pint without necessarily much attention given to complexity of flavour profile or consideration of apple variety. That is not to condemn any cider that presents as such – there are many great ciders that do this – but in the eyes of many consumers this is the stereotype of what cider is.

1976 – Cider duty reintroduced

It seems hard to believe for someone of my generation that less than 50 years ago there was no duty on cider at all. In fact, there had been no peacetime tax on cider since the Duke of Wellington repealed the duty burden in 1830.

However, on the back of cider's considerable post-war modernisation and growth, and no doubt egged on by a frustrated and already dutied beer industry, a full duty for cider was formally reintroduced in 1976. Thankfully, it was not undertaken with the same level of unwarranted access as the Cider Act of 1763, which led to rioting in the streets of Somerset and Gloucestershire, but nonetheless, the 22p duty on a gallon (4.8p per litre) of cider imposed overnight was a blow to a burgeoning industry, further forcing cider makers to undertake the 'value-engineering' practices already discussed.

This was a flat rate of duty between 1.2% and 8.5%. In 1996 a new bracket was introduced between 7.5% and 8.5% ABV at roughly +25% the standard rate, and in 2018 a further bracket between 6.9% and 7.5% ABV (at roughly +50% the standard rate). This latter band was brought in directly to tackle the cheap availability of 'white cider', but with no other mechanism than % ABV, any ciders, including those from smaller makers with an already high price point, were caught up as an unintended consequence.

Relatively speaking, an average strength cider (whatever that is) today will pay considerably less tax than a beer of the same ABV, because beer is taxed on a sliding scale linked to strength, not the banded flat rate that cider retains. This is to the chagrin of many within the brewing community who lament beer having to pay so much more to the Treasury.

What has justified cider being the recipient of this different treatment for the last 50-plus years? The answer is **apples**. The raw material for cider in Britain is predominantly bittersweet apples – specific varieties grown for the sole purpose of making cider – which contain high levels of tannin. Unlike brewers, who purchase their raw materials on the global spot market, there are considerable cost factors that come into play for cider makers using this fruit:

- It takes a number of years before the trees even start fruiting;

- This necessitates long contracts with growers – one can't change flavour profile easily;

- The high capital expenditure on equipment that is only used for a small part of the year;

- The support for rural economies where the cider makers operate.

This argument has become increasingly hard to justify, however, with an increasing proportion of the juice fermented into cider in the UK not being of indigenous origin, but mostly imported as AJC from Europe or further afield.

70hl duty exemption

A direct, constant and divisive relic of the reintroduction of duty that still holds massive sway over the actions of smaller cider makers today is the unprecedented 1,500 gallon duty exemption that HM Customs and Excise permitted to accompany the Finance Act 1976. With decimalisation, the figure was tweaked to 1,540 gallons or

7,000 litres, commonly referred to within legislative circles as 70 hectolitres (hl).

The purpose of the 70hl exemption was an incredibly pragmatic one – to prevent the tax officials from having to fend off imposing foliage as they wended their way down every single-track lane in South-East Devon to pay a visit to Farmer Brown who made three barrels of 'rough' every year to sell to unsuspecting townies on holiday at the farm gate. Forgive the multitude of clichés I managed to incorporate into a single sentence, but the essence remains entirely accurate. The cost benefit analysis showed it was a waste of time to visit the many hundreds of Farmer Browns located across the country.

This threshold has helped conserve many of these small farmhouse operations, as well as facilitating the establishment of hundreds of new producers whose intentions could be variously to monetise a hobby or to simply uphold a cultural heritage.

The 70hl duty exemption – a help and hindrance to small cider makers

In practical terms, too, this exemption, or rather the jump to the payment of a *full* rate of duty once over the 70hl threshold, is increasingly a cause for much debate. For those makers who only ever wish to make a small amount, this duty exemption is the mechanism that enables them to do this comfortably, viably and enjoyably. From this comes a broader consumer awareness of cider, the conservation and enhancement of orchards and some of the best ciders and perries made on the planet.

However, for anyone who aspires to grow their cider-making enterprise and provide a bill-paying salary for themselves (and maybe even for subsequent employees) and produce a volume of liquid that could grace shelves and bars all across the country, then the shift from duty exemption to full duty is a serious hurdle.

The jump in volume that is necessary to generate the same revenue while paying duty as when not having to involves a massive increase in expenditure on equipment, packaging and people. These very small duty-paying makers are, in effect, in direct competition with the biggest of big boys (paying the same rate of duty) but without any of the economies of scale and none of the duty discounts that the equivalent scale brewers receive through the Small Brewer's Duty Relief (SBDR) scheme.

✳

One of the perils of writing a book is that the moment it is published, it has the opportunity to be rendered obsolete in the blink of an eye. As far as this publication is concerned, given cider's painfully slow response to these matters, I reckon it's got a few years of relevance in its legs yet. But this section is the one that might fall by the wayside sooner rather than later owing to the aforementioned Alcohol Duty Review.

I think it highly likely that there will be a considerable change in the way all alcoholic drinks are dutied, especially if there is a recommendation to harmonise the duty systems of cider, beer, wines and spirits. The fallout from what such changes could be on cider is still entirely unknown. Harmonising duty will almost certainly increase the average duty paid by makers, but it could also provide an opportunity for a progressive duty system, like the SBDR, being implemented for cider, which could bring benefit for those aspirational makers. I'll just have to review all of this in the Second Edition! What is certain is that payment of duty, or not, will continue to play a major role in the fate of all British cider makers.

1980s – The cider revivalists

The decade in which technological fantasies started to become reality, even mainstream, was the 1980s. Think personal computers, mobile phones, CDs and, most importantly, Game Boys (spot of Tetris anyone?). It was during this decade that the lo-fi nature of the previous few decades started to recede in the rear view mirror as technology continued its inexorable march towards world domination.

But from this decade emerge the first vestiges of fear over the rampant pace of change. It could be said that the 1980s was the first decade that looked back as much as it did forward. This was a time when nostalgia emerged as a social and creative energy. We, as a Western society, had started to develop such wealth that we could afford to look back wistfully on a time with less work stress and a slower pace of life. This is somewhat romantic, of course, because for most people life up to the 1950s and 60s was bloody tough, especially in rural areas, with many having no running water or electricity.

The crucial thing is that this simplistic, pre-agro-industrialisation era was within living memory, or possibly even a lived experience. Many people began moving to rural areas from the urban grind to seek the good life, with many returning to the shires to raise their free-range children, just as they had been raised themselves. A few of these people discovered that cider was still being made the old way. Maybe this cider was rough and rustic scrumpy; maybe it was cider made with considerable skill and care like Lord

Scudamore and his *ciderists* of the 17th century; but it was there, just hanging on by its fingertips. In that sense cider was very much Britain's native wine, akin to the small farms of Piedmont or the Rhône Valley – making a bit for the family, a bit for the community, a bit for the labourer, and a bit for the odd unsuspecting tourist.

Alas, many cider makers, from farm operations up to regional-scale makers, had fallen by the wayside during the 20th century through acquisition and closure, squeezed competition on price and route to market by larger makers and continuing changes in consumers' tastes towards other drinks and other experiences.

This sense of a rural heritage being lost spurred into action a handful of long-time stalwarts and those beguiled by this drink's innate link to time and place. And so, the 1980s became the time of the great cider revival. One text encapsulated the virtually lost magic of cider (or should that be *cyder*): Roger French's *The History and Virtues of Cyder*. He wrote: 'Deep in the countryside something is stirring. Along the Marches of the Welsh Border, down in Devon and Somerset people are pulling from old barns forgotten pieces of strange machinery, large and old. They are tightening hoops on dry and dusty hogsheads. What is happening? They have rediscovered cyder.'

And boy did they! It was the passionate, devoted actions of these individuals that helped ensure that an entire heritage didn't disappear into a void along with Betamax. It would be inaccurate of me, however, to say that traditional cider (or cyder) making had entirely disappeared from its heartland areas by the 1980s. There were still a handful of devout exponents plugging on as they had always done, through thick and thin, through wars, floods and droughts. Some of these farmers just kept on going. The likes of John Hecks (Street, Somerset), Richard Sheppy (Bradford-on-Tone, Somerset), The Naish Brothers (West Pennard, Somerset), Derek Hartland (Tirley, Gloucestershire), Bob Luck (Benenden, Kent) and many others were still plying a trade, making and selling cider come the 1980s.

*Ivor and Susie
Dunkerton
– Organic cider
pioneers*

Of this new band of revivalists, a handful eschewed the lime-light and only ever made a small amount, their impact, importance and endeavours only known within traditional cider-making circles. The impact of the likes of Rose Grant (Rose's Cider, Dorset), Jean Nowell (Lyne Down Cider & Perry, Herefordshire) and Kevin Minchew (Minchew's Cyder, Gloucestershire) are still making an impact within their own regions today, if not always further afield. Other members of this revivalist cohort grew in volume and scale, with their ciders still prominent and enjoyed today. Crone's of Norfolk, Dunkerton's of Herefordshire (now Gloucestershire) and Gwatkin's of Herefordshire continue to be enjoyed at CAMRA festivals, as well as through regional and national retailers and pubs.

There are another three key individuals in this cider revival story, though their most telling contribution was not the making of cider. Firstly, we have Julian Temperley, a name known to many. He registered Burrow Hill Cider, in the Somerset Levels, in 1973 and continues to be a proud champion of extolling the virtues of cider packed to the brim with flavour, intensity and mystique.

It was his next venture that marks Julian's importance, however. In 1987 he started distilling his classic Somerset cider on two copper stills – Josephine and Fifi. In 1989 he was granted the UK's first ever full cider-distilling licence and has been distilling award-winning cider into Somerset Cider Brandy ever since. A drink with all of the calibre, essence and complexity as a Calvados or Lambig, Somerset Cider Brandy demonstrates the full range and capability of cider's use and has been the inspiration to all of the other cider-based spirits now available in Britain.

Secondly, we have Charles Martell, maker of fine cheese and based in the fine village of Dymock, Gloucestershire. Most famous for his Stinking Bishop cheese, and for his part in ensuring the survival of the Gloucester breed of cattle, Charles's greatest accomplishment (in my opinion) was the rediscovery of dozens of lost perry pear varieties in and around Gloucestershire during the 1980s and into the 1990s. It is thanks to his painstaking research and dogged determination that so many of these pear varieties are known and are being used and secured for future generations.

Julian Temperley assesses some of the Somerset Cider Brandy Co.'s finest

Last but not least, and crucial to this revival, was Alex Hill, based near Honiton, Devon. Although going on to become a cider maker of great repute, especially through his mastering of the bottle-fermenting technique under the Bollhayes brand, Alex's greatest contribution to the cider revival comes in establishing the cider equipment merchant Vigo.

By the early 80s there were no press manufacturers still operating in Britain. In order to get a press, one had to go to a farm sale in the hope of picking up a 1920s or 1930s press from the likes of Beare of Newton Abbot. Legend has it that a cider maker bought up all of the old presses in the South-West and destroyed them all in an attempt to fend off competition from new entrants into the marketplace. One never knows whether these fables have any truth. Much like the rumour that white cider was actually made with onion skins back in the 1990s, everything should be taken with a pinch of salt. Anyway, Vigo heralded a profusion of new equipment providers who democratised the access to mills, presses, filters, bottling machines, etc., all state of the art and with a price to suit every pocket.

The impact of these revivalists is still being keenly felt today. The cider makers pushing the drive for real cider are either those revivalists themselves, still valiantly plugging away, or those directly taught or inspired by those pioneers. We salute you all!

1986 – National Fruit and Cider Institute closes

Imagine this: a bespoke facility, dedicated to the pursuit of improving the scientific understanding of a long-standing alcoholic beverage, packed full of the finest technological, microbiological, horticultural and biochemical minds in the world. What am I talking about? UC Davis in California, or the Australian Wine Research Institute in Adelaide? No, I'm talking about the National Fruit and Cider Institute (NFCI) of Long Ashton, Bristol.

Established in 1903, the NFCI was developed in response to cider making starting to become a commercial venture, rather than simply a farmhouse enterprise, and sought to improve every step of the cider-making process. Changing its name to the Long Ashton Research Station (LARS) in 1912 when it was incorporated into the University of Bristol's Department of Agricultural and Horticultural Research, it was for the next 50 years the world leader in cider science.

By the late 1960s LARS had undertaken the majority of fundamental research critical to creating controlled, replicable cider:

- A strong understanding was developed of the chemical composition of different types of juice – sugars, acids, tannins, esters, etc;
- The identification of key yeast and bacteria, their impacts and control methods had been established;
- Maladies were understood, and prevented, thanks to improved microbiological assessment techniques and judicious SO_2 management;
- The full development of knowledge on bush tree growing, pollination and mechanical orchard management.

Cider-making research in action

Up to this point LARS was still receiving funding from the government for its academic research. However, from the late 1960s it had to start bidding for funding, and it became increasingly difficult to justify public funds for cider research. So many of the fundamental components of cider making had already been established that, by 1972, there were only six cider-focused researchers remaining at LARS.

In an attempt to keep research going, LARS approached the cider makers themselves to ask for financial support, and so from 1974 until 1985 two research posts were funded directly by the NACM. However, larger cider makers had by now invested in the considerable development of in-house laboratories, technicians, product development and sensory assessments and were making cider the way they wanted. As a result, the NFCI, including all cider research, was finally wound up in 1986, although the NACM continued to fund a cider pomology support post. In 2003 LARS was closed for good.

So much of what we know about the intricacies of growing tannic apples and perry pears, of their properties, and of their nature of fermentation, maturation and stabilisation is directly owed to the fine folk at the NFCI undertaking research during those halcyon years. We have so much to be thankful for, and to be proud of. Key figures, such as Andrew Lea, Liz Copas and Keith Goverd, who have done so much to aid the development of smaller cider makers over the last 30 years, are a direct product of this system.

But there is also a considerable regret on my part that such research is no longer undertaken. It feels that with a new, latent interest in the production of cider on these isles, there is a greater desire than ever to understand the intricacies of cider and perry making. There are so many questions that need answering. How will the growing of apples for cider change with global warming? What *actually* causes mouse, the most heinous of taste faults? Why *did* my perry taste of sausages that one time?

1988 – CAMRA APPLE committee established

The roots of cider campaigning through CAMRA go all the way back to the mid-1970s when cider started to occasionally find its way to CAMRA festivals in London. At the Acton Festival, in the summer of 1974, the end of the night drink of choice was Horace Lancaster's Countryman Cider, which, allegedly, made complete fools of the drinkers more used to the gentle, assuaging sensations derived from the Mild and Best Bitter on offer.

Into the 1980s cider and perry started to appear at more and more CAMRA festivals thanks to the actions of the likes of Mick Lewis, Jon Hallam and Sara Hicks, Dick Budgen and David Kitton. Such was the level of increasing interest from CAMRA members that by the 1983 Great British Beer Festival (GBBF) in Birmingham it warranted its very own bar.

David Kitton's role was of great significance thanks to his endeavours to find and catalogue the last remaining farmhouse cider makers, and to locate the newly establishing revivalists. This list was originally published under the name of *The Traditional Cider Directory* through Virgin Books, but didn't gain enough traction and was eventually brought in house, and thus the first *Good Cider Guide* was published by CAMRA in 1987.

Finding ciders to stock at these festivals was no easy task. The buyers for the festival, although armed with David Kitton's listing, would also have to use the telephone directory or just follow their noses down increasingly narrow lanes in Devon and Somerset. Most of these makers relied upon farm-gate sales to local loyalists and the odd smattering of tourists.

Mick Lewis recounts some of these early visits. 'I remember going to visit Vickery Cider in Somerset, where the instruction was to head down the A303, turn left and keep going! And then there was Hisbeer's Farm, near Chard. There was the tiniest little sign saying cider for sale. The farm was very much a family affair, run by two brothers and their mum and dad. They had really good,

Cider advocacy in action at the 2000 Stockport CAMRA Beer & Cider Festival

really dry cider. Their accents were so broad that when the dad told a joke I had to guess when the punchline was!'

It took until 1988, however, before cider cemented its place firmly, formally and finally into the heart of CAMRA. Mick Lewis pointed out that CAMRA had been making money from cider and perry for years through the festival bars, but not giving anything back to this small and struggling industry. Along with Ed Fahey, Mick proposed a motion to create a committee whose sole remit was to oversee real cider and perry's advocacy. The motion was passed and The Apple & Pear Produce Liaison Executive (APPLE) was created.

The greatest and most long-standing result of the establishment of APPLE was the creation of a definition of Real Cider, in 1990, which was then formalised in 2003. This was based on the following primary factors:

- Made from fresh apple juice – not from concentrate;
- 100% juice – no gross chaptalisation and/or dilution;
- No filtering (for clarification);
- No pasteurising and no sterile filtering (for stabilisation).

Even if not with any legal basis, and with an increasing lack of enforceability for the last 10 years or so, this standard has been the only consumer-facing definition for ciders and perries that seeks to go beyond the mass-produced sector. In the face of great commodification of cider during the 1980s and well into the 2000s, this definition ensured that consumers were able to have a level of confidence that the ciders at CAMRA festivals and in CAMRA-approved pubs were not the cider equivalent of lifeless, inert lagers. These real ciders were the equivalent of real ale – fresh and 'live'.

This definition, and the cider and perry that has been advocated through it over the course of the last 30-plus years, has had an incredibly positive impact upon the small/traditional/farmhouse cider community in Britain. It has showcased the fact that cider can come in different formats (still rather than carbonated), can come with different sensory experiences (boldly tannic or zingily sharp rather than ubiquitously middling) and can be of a different level of sweetness (bone dry rather than majorly back sweetened).

It has showcased that cider can, and is, made not only in the classic heartland regions of the South-West, Three Counties and Kent, but also across these islands, with each different region expressing unique characteristics. And crucially, it has provided an outlet for some considerable volumes of cider sales for many smaller producers, providing viability in a challenging marketplace.

The real differences between cask ale and cider

It is not to say that CAMRA's championing hasn't come without some challenge, disagreement and hullaballoo, however. The assertion by some that real (ostensibly farmhouse) cider is an equivalent to real (cask-conditioned) ale is not something I have always agreed with. For me, they are completely different beasts.

Cask-conditioned beers control the actions of wild yeast and bacteria through the boiling of the wort and containing of long chain sugars and lazy yeasts such that they can harbour safe and stable residual sweetness. Crucially, cask-conditioned beer is the

result of the primary fermentation undertaken on demand, ensuring brightness and freshness of flavour and short lifespan. Finally, there is a well understood and respected heritage of properly cellaring these beers to ensure they reach the consumer in tip-top condition.

Minimally intervened cider, historically and today, is a completely different drink in terms of production, appreciation and consumption. Classically, cider is drawn straight from the barrel – still, dry and bold from six months plus of maturation. Once removed from the safe(r) confines of its air-minimised environment, this cider had a limited lifespan – the microflora inherent within the cider, plus that which it has suddenly come into contact with, will begin to make its (generally negative) presence felt on the cider.

Traditionally, this didn't matter so much. Cider was mostly consumed by the local folk, labourers, and maybe a bit for the local pub. The key is that it was drunk quickly. Once cider started to be distributed and sold all around the country, thanks to the likes of Bulmers, Westons and Showerings in the early 20th century, means and methods were established to ensure that the cider was still in a fit state for consumption when it arrived in Leeds, London, Swansea or Middlesbrough.

The advent of the polypin (rigid plastic, 40 pint, vented pressure vessel with a tap for serving) provided the opportunity for smaller makers to easily shift chunky volumes of their 'live' ciders to pubs near and far, as well to the increasing number of real ale (and cider/perry) festivals being hosted by CAMRA all around the country.

If the polypin of cider was transported from farm to festival, or pub, with haste and care, properly cellared and consumed quickly, then this was, and still is, the most joyous way to experience the best of real cider. Sometimes, it would have been deliberately conditioned to go dry and spritzy, but mostly it would have had added sugar (or saccharin) to be presented as a sweet(er), or sometimes simply bone dry, as Pomona intended.

But without the cellaring knowledge or respect of cask-conditioned beer, the lack of conditioning knowledge/control (if any) from the makers, and the sheer will of the inherent microflora to continually convert sugars, acids and alcohols with unintended consequences, these live ciders often did not (and still do not) provide a pleasant drinking experience. This gave rise to the advent of the Bag in Box (BIB) as a preferred method of packaging for smaller makers looking to shift volume, providing a longer lifespan through exclusion of air when drawing down, but also frequently through pasteurisation.

I want to clarify here that I am a passionate advocate for 'live' cider on draught, whether it be conditioned, bone dry, or sweet. I am also a fan of full-juice pasteurised/carbonated keg ciders, focusing as much on the quality of the raw materials, method of production, lack of faults and accessibility to the consumer more than whether the cider is live or not. I believe all of the diverse types, styles and presentations of cider, on draught or packaged, have their part to play in engaging with consumers, old and new, in this modern world of cider.

CAMRA is not averse to change, however, even if under slightly controversial circumstances. Much to the consternation of real cider and perry stalwarts, a motion was passed at the 2015 AGM allowing flavoured ciders and perries to be considered real, as long as the flavour was natural in origin, fresh and pure, rather than processed in some way. So, today strawberry can be found alongside Stoke Red at many festivals, although some festival bar managers do not wish to advocate those drinks.

In 2019 the APPLE Committee was disbanded, with all cider activities now running centrally through committees that also deal with beer issues, with designated cider champions running from top to bottom. This process of change has culminated in the development of a new definition of real cider and perry – published in May 2021 – that is easy to follow and that makes sense across all dispense methods. It is designed to reflect the changes in production and consumption of cider over the last 40 years. We will review this in the next chapter.

Regardless of challenges and changes, there is no doubt that the plight of smaller cider makers in Britain has been considerably advanced over the course of the last half century as a result of CAMRA's actions. Cheers!

1990s – The rise and fall of the alcopop

The 1990s was the decade that restraint forgot. Generation X were on a full rampage of living it large, whether it be 'ladettes' smashing back pints of Lager, all-nighters at Super Clubs or lads on tour in Magaluf.

What is the state of cider in Britain during this time? Not great, if truth be told. There had been some volume growth since the late 1980s, but this had been driven largely through value ciders, mainstream ciders and, most notoriously, white ciders. By 1995 cider had reached its zenith of low-value perception, with the increasing prevalence of large PET bottles (up to 3l), of a high-alcohol content (usually 7.5%) being sold at low prices in supermarkets and convenience stores. Still to this day, White Lightening is often quoted in a painful/wistful recollection of a misspent youth.

Out of this gustatory tundra, and as a great exemplification of the excessive trashiness of this time, emerged the development of the alcopop. These beverages, also known within the drinks industry by the slightly less emotionally charged Ready to Drink (RTD), developed at a time when the speed and ease of alcohol consumption was paramount. Bacardi Breezer had been around since 1993, but the big splash came in 1995 with the launch of Two Dogs and Hooper's Hooch.

It was the latter that caught the hearts and minds of its target consumers, namely young people. Lurid of colour, childish of graphic and alluring of name (Alcoholic Lemonade) it was a palpable hit. Later, there came Vault, Tilt, VK, Red Square, Reef and WKD, and by 1996 the term 'alcopop' was being widely used, normally attached to sensationalised headlines in the Red Tops – 'Alcopop Drug Barons' and 'Purge on "Pop" Booze' spring to mind.

There was an inevitable backlash. In the 1996 Budget, then-chancellor, Kenneth Clarke increased the duty on such drinks by 40%, which massively hastened their decline. The drinks industry, whose reputation had been battered, responded through its self-funded responsible drinking arm, The Portman Group. Although established in 1989, it was only in the aftermath of the alcopop debacle in 1996 that it established its code of practice.

In the late 90s and into the early 2000s we saw the emergence of a handful of ciders that sought to emulate alcopops. Some of these were of British origin, but the brands they drove hardest were Swedish. These drinks were defined by their sweetness, their ease of drinking and their remarkable similarity to alcopops in taste and design, but without the stigma. Frequently, they came with other flavours, which ensured that they weren't taxed as a cider, but as we have already seen, they could bear the name. But these drinks' prominence would have to wait until 2006.

2006 – The Magner's effect

If you're old enough to have been of drinking age in 2006, you'll remember a few things about that summer. Firstly, it was hot; ruddy hot. Secondly, the FIFA World Cup was being played in Germany during June and July. These two factors led to large numbers of people heading to pubs, and into pub gardens especially, during these months, and into the school holidays. Little did the drinks trade know, but there was a new(ish) drink that was to provide the liquid soundtrack to this summer of sun. That drink was Magner's Irish Cider.

Initially launched into the UK market in 2005, the positive but measured consumer response led parent company C&C to undertake a major roll of the apple-themed dice. Armed with a marketing kitty the size of the GDP of a small Central American nation, Magner's exploded onto the TV screens, billboards and inside covers of magazines in the spring of 2006 showcasing their cider as being something fun, convivial and to be drunk by men *and* women. To finish off, drinkers were told to consume this playful, fun cider *over ice*. And then all hell broke loose.

Magner's didn't invent the concept of serving over ice (surely that was Withnail and I?) but they did execute its full potential absolutely perfectly: not only was ice appealing during a hot summer, but it also became an intimate part of the *ritual* of drinking that cider (and subsequent ciders). This notion of ritual is something cask ale has in oodles – the hand pull, the head, the cling, etc. – but it's one that cider lacks.

The Magner's effect, as it has subsequently become known, led to a slew of 'me too' brands from other cider makers, ensuring that fresh, juicy, sweet ciders would dominate the category for the next five years. It also meant it was nigh on impossible to go into a pub and order a cider and **not** be asked if I wanted ice in that. Ultimately, it helped boosted the total volume sales of cider in Britain by 50% in the space of the three years.

It also kickstarted a positive, fun, vibrant association with cider for many drinkers in the UK, less tarnished or burdened with preconceptions or memories of what had come before. This was a fresh start. Many consumers went on a journey to investigate cider more deeply and more thoroughly, resulting not only in the 'big boys' benefiting but *all* cider makers, from top to bottom. I'm sure CAMRA's records would attest to a considerable uptick in cider's presence at festival bars post-2006, and certainly the number of smaller producers that established or grew considerably in this timeframe would attest to the continual impact of the Magner's Effect.

From a category dynamic point of view, Magner's greatest legacy is that it expedited the growth of flavoured ciders. As we saw previously, the alcopop category was taxed into oblivion in the previous decade, but with many consumers still demanding an easy, sugary hit, and with cider being on trend, it was a natural progression for consumers to seek out these drinks, and cider makers duly obliged.

The new wave of millennial drinkers that soaked up Magner's was characterised by their lust for exploration and trying new things: especially if they were sweet, juicy and cold. After a short-lived dalliance with pear cider (made primarily from imported dessert pear juice concentrate), consumers turned their attention to the emergence of the fruity flavoured offerings from the Scandinavian brands, with Kopparberg at the fore, quickly followed by a swathe of UK-produced copycat versions.

These drinks make up a significant proportion of the UK cider category today, much to the chagrin of many makers and drinkers of more classic styles. Proponents of flavoured ciders will say that these drinks act as a gateway to the broader cider category, but I'm less certain that this is the case, and it is far more likely for them to interchange with those RTDs that cling on in the marketplace, or even a vodka and coke. What we do know is that flavoured ciders are here to stay and we'll delve a little deeper into their role and opportunity in the next chapter.

2007 – Punk IPA is born

If there is one drinks trend that is synonymous with the 21st century thus far, and of a generational effort to break with the past and seek a newly imagined future, it has to be craft beer. As Pete Brown so eloquently established in his book *Craft: An Argument*, 'the term craft beer is completely undefinable, hopelessly misunderstood and absolutely essential.' For many beer drinkers, and for many CAMRA members, the craft beer movement was, and still is, a challenge to understand and accept. Craft beer is largely pasteurised and kegged under pressure (although there are many craft brewers that do produce in cask, too), it can come with a brashness, a healthy dollop of ludicrousness, and quite often with a range of poorly brewed beers from a technical point of view.

But this movement, and those breweries than sit within this undefinable category, have produced more excitement, more prosperity and more landmark brands over the course of the last 15 years that any other drinks category, and there can be no denying that craft beer has changed the landscape of long drinks consumption in the UK. Inspired by the smaller, independent breweries of the USA (with the likes of Sierra Nevada, Stone Brewing, Goose Island, Dogfish Head, etc. to the fore), who were railing against the blandness of corporate American beer by producing bold, intensely hopped re-imaginings of the traditional styles, such as India Pale Ale (IPA), a handful of young brewers in the UK took note.

One of them, Martin Dickie, teamed up with his old school chum, James Watt, in 2007 to found the most influential, and controversial, craft brewery in the UK – BrewDog. Having already gained experience of experimenting with boldly hopped beers at Thornbridge (Jaipur anyone?), it was BrewDog's modern take on the IPA style as the flagship beer that hit the mark with so many people – Punk IPA was born.

The flavour and aroma was intense with Nelson Sauvin hops from New Zealand delivering a tropical lusciousness and a spiky

bitter finish that good old British Fuggles could only dream of. Crucially, the proudly subversive, counterculture branding appealed to those who wanted something different – less corporate, less establishment, the path less followed. This was then backed up by extreme beers (the world's highest ABV served out of a stuffed squirrel), the outlandish brewing techniques (ageing at the bottom of the sea) and the stunts (driving a tank down Camden High Street).

The epitome of this ethos and attitude was to place Punk IPA into 330ml cans. Not that BrewDog was the first craft brewer to pack its beer into a size of can more usually associated with a soft drink. No, that accolade goes to Oskar Blues' Dale's Pale Ale in 2002. But from a British perspective this was revelatory, creating a whole new experience, and its impact upon beer presentation has been immense. Jonny Bright of the Hereford Beer House says, 'In 2015 I opened a bottle shop and now I run a can shop.'

There are plenty of people within the craft beer community, and beyond, who question BrewDog's status in the craft beer community thanks to their considerable volume, private equity investment and recent accusations of a culture of fear within the organisation. There can be no denying, however, that BrewDog, with Punk IPA as its flagship, changed modern British beer and contemporary British drinking habits in three key ways:

- Firstly, it spawned the craft aesthetic – bold, brash, fun, innovative in terms of presentation and liquid. It made 'old fashioned' drinks like beer, gin and rum (and then bread, biscuits, ketchup, etc.) viable and valued through a new language and a new style;

- Secondly, it drove an increase in the value perception of beer (and those subsequent drinks and other foodstuffs) such that it was viable for small-scale, bespoke businesses to service this demand – breweries, bars, bottle shops, festivals;

- Thirdly, it helped facilitate a whole new drinker – the 'curious consumer'. They seek bold flavours, new experiences and, increasingly, these are not limited to beer.

It is precisely these consumers, this increase in value perception and this type of presentation that has, and will continue to, become increasingly important for cider. To engage, connect and to be relevant to a whole new demographic of drinkers who were not previously consuming cider provides an incredible opportunity to increase the volume, value and vitality to this traditional drink.

2020 – Covid-19 pandemic

Firstly, to everyone who works in hospitality, if you have emerged out the other side of this period with your job, business and sanity intact, I commend you. That could only be attributable to a lot of furlough, effort and stress.

Make no bones about it, Covid-19 has devastated many cider businesses. A small number have closed (Crazy Dave's and Harlesden spring to mind), while others have clung on through begging, borrowing or returning to other forms of employment. That isn't to say that beer and spirits have had an easy ride, but they do have the benefit of their raw materials being purchased to demand, with the establishment of production undertaken to order. Cider, of course, is *made*, rather than *brewed* and the raw material for cider (i.e., apples) is harvested once a year and classically milled, pressed and fermented into cider for long-term maturation. It could also be the case for some cider makers that once the apples are harvested, they are stockpiled in cold storage, or converted into concentrate, for use throughout the year as required.

Either way, by the time of the 2020 Northern Hemisphere harvest all cider makers found themselves sitting on quite a large pile of cider, or apples/juice waiting to be converted into cider, that had not been able to be sold as per usual. The extra sales seen within retail, although significant, were not enough to make up for the crushing loss of the pub route to market. The knock-on effect of this was that there was considerably reduced empty tank capacity, which in turn meant that less fruit was harvested and less cider made. The trickle-down effect of this into British agriculture was significant, especially considering that the cider industry uses 45% of all apples grown in the UK.

Cider also over-indexed on the significance of the challenges provided by Covid-19: a significant proportion of the volume that is normally sold in any given year is at summer festivals, events and fairs, none of which were able to happen on any scale. All in all, it's has been a bit of a rough time.

But out of significant adversity there has emerged a glimmer of hope, innovation and some exciting new trends. And it could be argued that Covid-19 may have advanced the pace of these changes.

With the pub experience not being an option, people decided to direct their discretionary spending on drinks through online portals. Sales through online beer shops and beer subscription boxes soared and cider didn't miss out either. Established web shops saw their sales explode, encouraging a raft of new e-commerce start-ups, as well as B2B businesses quickly adapting and changing their models to accommodate the B2C opportunity. Cider makers themselves, not always known for their willingness to adapt to modern trading opportunities, capitalised upon the reality that online sales were going to make up the majority of their trading during the uncertain times. The result – an entirely new route to market for many producers, and an entirely new opportunity for consumers.

By navigating a new space, place and method of drinks purchasing, these curious consumers were able to find, embrace and explore a huge range of smaller brands that they had not previously encountered in major retailers and pubs. This exploration helped create an energy, dynamism and fervour for bottled and canned ciders from craft producers that has not been seen in the UK before.

Whether expedited through the above sequence of events, or a trend that was imminent regardless of Covid-19, UK craft cider makers blossomed in 2020 and into 2021 by releasing a whole raft of exciting products into the market. These have been a mixture of entirely new, limited edition liquids, and/or the rebranding and repositioning of pre-existing brands. What they all shared was an aspiration for being more highly valued, and to appeal to these aforementioned curious consumers.

Allied to this greater visibility of, and accessibility to, characterful cider than ever before, a huge number of online value added activities started to emerge to help plug the social and experiential void left by pubs being closed. The emergence of online tutored tasting sessions, monthly cider clubs and virtual festivals were all something that helped people navigate the social-inhibiting fallout from Covid-19. More than that, however, they also presented a new and unique way to provide entertaining and informative content and experiences available to participants, regardless of where they lived in the UK, or even around the globe.

As a result of all of this, even as we emerge from the impact of Covid-19 and something approaching normality returns, these trends, these activities and these methods of purchasing cider will all remain. Remarkably, I think cider will emerge from this unprecedented time as a stronger, more visible, more accessible and more exciting proposition.

THE LANDSCAPE OF MODERN BRITISH CIDER

The Big Numbers

Thus far we have discovered that there have been a multitude of events, people, actions, legislation, products and fads that are still impacting upon the way cider is made, understood, consumed and taxed today. But just what is the landscape of modern British cider?

Access to data isn't always easy, but thankfully we have a great overview in the form of the annual Westons Cider Report (WCR). This pulls together retail, on-trade and shopper information from various data providers, in nice, bitesize, publicly available chunks. The following numbers are mostly quoted from the 2018, 2019, 2020 and 2021 iterations of the WCR.

It is pertinent to point out, of course, that this data is reflective of the pre-Covid era and highlights broader trends. Much like any other drinks category, 2020, and at least the first half of 2021, is not reflective of normal times. It remains to be seen what normal will look like as we head into 2022 and beyond, and there's no doubt that new trends will emerge as a result of Covid-19.

Who Drinks Cider?

Well, quite a lot of people, actually. In 2019 786m litres of cider was sold in Britain, with a total value of £3.1 billion. Both these figures are paradoxically huge and yet relatively minor at the same. Sure, Britain accounts for 37.5% of global cider sales, but this figure was once much greater – its reduction a result of cider markets around the world exploding into life while remaining relatively static on the home front. At the same time in Britain, cider amounts for less than 10% of all alcohol consumed – the smallest of drinks categories, barring RTDs (alcopops).

Similarly, cider's value, sitting at £3.1 billion, is approximately three times the size of the UK fishing industry – a proud bastion of national identity – yet this figure is dwarfed by beer's value of £14.1 billion.

Around the globe, cider was, and still is, viewed predominately as a feminine drink, with beer encapsulating the essence of masculinity. Britain is the only market in the world where, during the latter part of the 20th century, cider was seen as a masculine drink, largely thanks to Strongbow and a slew of subsequent brands that evoked the value of 'strong'.

The Magner's Effect served to change this, however, presenting cider as something fun, mixed-sex and accessible. The subsequent rise of flavoured ciders has increasingly driven the appeal of cider to women, with the spilt of total volume consumed sitting at 53% male and 47% female.

Geographically, cider in Britain is truly a nationally consumed drink. This isn't particularly surprising to many folk, but it does have a significant point of difference from the other 'Old World' producing markets, such as France, Spain or Germany. In these nations the consumption of cider is almost exclusively linked to the specific areas of heritage and production – Normandy/Brittany in France, Asturias/Basque Country in Spain, and Hessen in Germany.

Although cider in Britain is predominantly produced in rural areas, its consumption is ubiquitous across all parts of the British Isles and Northern Ireland, and from a total volume consumption point of view, would not be considered to be a rural experience anymore.

Here's a whopping great stat for you:

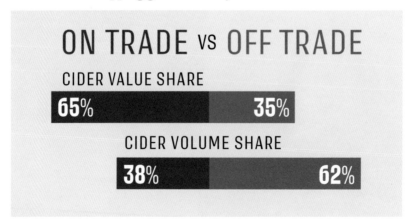

ON TRADE vs OFF TRADE

CIDER VALUE SHARE

65%   35%

CIDER VOLUME SHARE

38%   62%

Festivals, cider and sunshine – for many it's the perfect mix

Drinking booze is now considerably more likely to take place at home rather than down the pub, and with that has come entire societal change. The low value, relative to the volume, in the off-trade is demonstrative of the low average price point that the consumer has to pay in order to get their cider satisfaction. I categorially do not want cider to be elitist or unavailable to those folk not rolling in cash, but there is a line beyond which the reputation, and viability of production, of this drink is severely impacted upon.

✳

Cider's greatest emotional association for many drinkers is the sunshine. To observe the sales data trends around that first warm and sunny weekend of spring of any given year is to witness the most incredible, skyscraper-like, vertical shoot of the line, represen-ting the several million drinkers turning back to cider after the winter hibernation.

Cider's association with summer, (relative) warmth, the outdoors, camping, festivals and good vibes is a wonderful boon for the category. But this over-indexing link to six months of the year makes things rather tricky for makers. I'm sure brewers will see a down tick in Lager sales in the winter, but how many of those drinkers actually bid fond farewell to those styles of drink for half the year, just because the weather has gone a bit nippy?

Who Makes Cider?

So, this is the tricky bit. Trying to get hold of publicly available data detailing the number of producers and their volumes is an arduous task, fraught with Indiana Jones-levels of leaping about and mystery solving. It should be a reasonably simple question to answer: how many commercial, registered, selling cider makers are there in Britain today? The answer = 🤷 .

This information isn't being captured by the NACM, it's not being divulged by HMRC and it's not being formally coordinated by any singular individual or organisation. The exceedingly handy 2020 *Cider Manual* had a good stab at trying to deduce this figure, and their survey said that there were 368 cider makers. This figure, of course, only represents those who wished to be featured in this publication, and such is the ability for cider makers to obscure themselves that the *Cider Manual* team were never going to track down everyone. I've featured an extra 20 or so makers later in this publication, and with a bit of extrapolation, one could easily deduce that, not including hobbyists, community groups and tax dodgers, **there are probably nigh on 500 commercial cider makers in Great Britain and Northern Ireland**.

Bigger-scale cider making

Of greater interest and pertinence in understanding how the construct of the industry impacts upon the ability of cider makers to operate is their distribution by *scale* rather than the sheer *number* of producers. This is where things get really tough in terms of available data, with many of the largest makers not being particularly willing to divulge the prime cuts of information.

The spread of British cider makers by their annual volume of production is effectively on a logarithmic curve. We start with one behemoth, commanding just about half of all the cider sold in Britain. Next we jump to no more than a dozen big makers who, between them, command a decent proportion of the rest of UK volume. The NACM states that its members account for around 85% of all the volume produced in the UK, but this figure excludes a handful of larger makers who are non-members, and who undoubtedly make up a fair proportion of the remaining 15%.

We then sweep down a ski slope of not much before hitting a mass of small and micro producers at the bottom of the hill. To my knowledge, there are only two or three cider makers operating in the 3–24 million litres range of annual volume production of cider.

I know that 3 million litres would be considered gargantuan for those at the micro end of things, but to put that into perspective, it accounts for 0.38% of all cider sold in the UK in 2019.

Smaller-scale cider making

In British brewing, proud names such as Youngs, Thwaites, Theakstons and Arkells, and many others, showcase that regional (often still family owned) brewers can compete with the largest brewers in the marketplace. The growth of a similar category of regional cider makers is an absolutely fundamental step in the drive for cider to become a fully-fledged, dynamic, diverse, healthy and prosperous category.

The final nugget that the *Cider Manual* provides us is that 61% of the makers they featured in the book identified as being under the 70hl limit. Let's assume that every one of those 224 producers made 70hl on the nose in 2020 (which wouldn't be the case, but run with it anyway), that would account for a total volume of 1.57 million litres – the precise average volume of Strongbow Original sold *every day* in 2019. Food for thought.

It would be entirely emblematic of cider's lack of self-esteem to simply shrug one's shoulders at these numbers, to feel that with such low visibility and presence in the marketplace, how could smaller cider makers ever grow and compete with the bigger makers? As previously mentioned, to aspire to grow in volume is certainly admirable, and indeed crucial for cider to achieve its full potential. But volume alone isn't going to be the key – it's going to be the value associated with the products.

Take British wine, for example. It is heralded as a burgeoning bastion of quality British drinks, wins trophies at international competitions, gets drunk on British Airways First Class and has an increasingly valuable tourism industry based around it. Yet, in 2019 GB-produced wine accounted for only 0.52% of all the wine consumed in the UK.

Volume isn't everything, but belief, passion, professionalism, understanding and value perception are.

Regardless of scale, aspiration is key

Categorising Cider by Segment

The data generated by the aforementioned agencies is based on recorded numbers – it is unambiguous and factual. As well as wishing to understand the *who, how* and *where* with regards to cider, naturally we all want to know the *what*, too. Cider typically gets lumped together into different segments for sales data analysis. The nature of these groupings, and which brands are placed within them, are based less upon apple variety, production methodology or flavour profile and more about value perception, alcohol content, pack presentation, mode of consumption and level of advertising spend.

This is how the WCR 2018 has grouped these segments:

Value White

- **ABV range**: above 6%
- **Reason for purchase**: 'bang for your buck'
- **Where sold**: retail only
- **Pack type**: Large PET bottle (normally blue coloured)
- **Description**: often the cheapest unit of alcohol to be purchased on the high street, it has long been the focus of opprobrium from the health lobby, labelled over the last decade as being akin to heroin
- **Classic brands**: Frosty Jack's and Omega

Value Amber

- **ABV range**: under 6%
- **Reason for purchase**: 'cheap and accessible'
- **Where sold**: retail only – branded or own label
- **Pack type**: large PET bottle
- **Description**: cheap, unpretentious cider, easily available to all
- **Classic brands**: Crumpton Oaks and Crofters

Mainstream

- **ABV range**: 4–5.5%
- **Reason for purchase**: 'easy drinking, sessionable ciders'
- **Where sold**: retail and pubs
- **Pack type**: in cans for retail, often multipacks, and on draught in the pub
- **Description**: mainstream ciders account for the majority of large volume brands who enjoy high advertising spend and high brand awareness
- **Classic brands**: Strongbow and Thatchers Gold

Premium

- **ABV range**: 4–5.5%
- **Reason for purchase**: 'fun, fruity and youthful aesthetics'
- **Where sold**: retail and pubs
- **Pack type**: typically packed in bottles for the off-trade and on-trade, but with an increasing prominence on draught for the on-trade
- Description: increasingly dominated by flavoured ciders, these drinks enjoy high advertising spend and high brand awareness
- **Classic brands**: Kopparberg and Rekorderlig

Crafted

- **ABV range**: 4–8.4%
- **Reason for purchase**: 'exploration and enhanced taste'
- **Where sold**: retail and pubs
- **Pack type**: typically packed in bottles for the off-trade and on-trade, and available on draught for the on-trade in keg or Bag In Box (BIB)
- **Description**: ciders presented as traditional or modern and made by 'independent' producers, often with heritage and provenance cues
- **Classic brands**: Weston's Vintage, Aspall Draught

Minimum Unit Pricing

The creation and intention of this categorisation by segment was, and still is, only for the benefit of analysing broader trends and has never been for the benefit of the drinker, to arm them with information that will tell them how any given cider will taste.

What these categories do facilitate, however, is to shine a spotlight onto the overarching commodification of cider – how such a high percentage of the volume of cider sold in Britain is as cheap as chips. Now, far be it from me to deny lower income folk the opportunity to get alcohol at affordable prices – everybody deserves to enjoy a cider. I can't help but feel, however, that cider has become overly synonymous in the public consciousness with a cheap source of alcohol.

Certainly, the devolved governments of Britain, under pressure from the health lobby to reduce the nation's overall intake of alcohol and specifically to tackle harmful drinking, think that there should be a basic Minimum Unit Price (MUP) for alcoholic drinks. Set at 50p per unit of alcohol (a 4.5% pint of cider contains roughly 2.5 units), Scotland and Wales have already implemented MUP in May 2018 and March 2020, respectively, with Westminster having a very close look at this mechanism for England, too.

There is, of course, not much chance of a pint of cider being sold in a pub for less than £1.25. It's in the retail rather than the pub environment where the greatest impact of MUP is felt. At the time of writing, in England I can purchase a 2.5 litre bottle of 7.5% white cider from a supermarket for £3.70, which equates to a tad less than 20p per unit of alcohol. If MUP were to apply, the lowest retail price would be £9.37. One can also purchase a multipack of 18 × 440ml cans of a mainstream cider for £10, equating to 28p per unit of alcohol. If MUP were to apply, this would have to rise to at least £17.82.

The full ramifications of this market-based rather than tax-based measure on consumption habits are yet to fully reveal themselves. Early indications from Scotland and Wales suggest an overall reduction in consumption of alcohol, but what will be interesting to learn over time is whether consumers are more willing to trade across to ciders from smaller makers (which will naturally sit above the MUP threshold because of cost of production) as the price differential between them and white/value/mainstream ciders is reduced. A trend of drinking less but drinking better, something already observed by the growth of the crafted segment, may well be accelerated under MUP. We shall have to wait and see.

Categorising Cider by Type

The only other set of distinctions that are used by these agencies, and by the industry and broader trade, to analyse and communicate the category, is that based upon the type of cider. Here they are:

- **Apple**
- **Pear**
- **Fruit**

Here in Britain we have a commercial cider-making industry over 150 years old, we have the world's largest market and have access to some of the finest apples and orchards, and all we have to show for this heritage, this investment, and this diversity is 'apple', 'pear' and 'fruit'. It's all rather uninspiring.

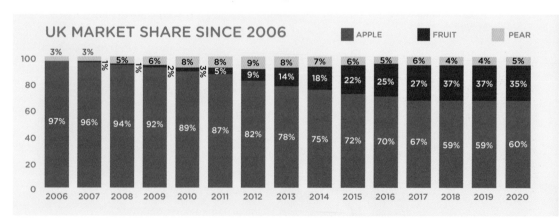

Apple

To describe a whole segment of cider as 'apple' is like describing a type of wine as 'grape' or beer as 'malt'. I know that is to differentiate it from the fermentation of pear and, more importantly, those ciders that are flavoured, but it really does serve to highlight the paucity of descriptors.

Beyond maybe a description of the level of sweetness on the front of the label, there is nothing else within the wider domain to describe any differences between 'apple' ciders. Drinks within the 'apple' segment could be acid driven or tannic driven, they could have undergone a special fermentation or maturation process, or they could be inextricably linked to a particular place.

The decline of orchards

What is certain is that we find ourselves in a time of flux from an apple-growing perspective. A drive down the winding roads of Herefordshire or Somerset might afford a glimpse of a number of modern bush orchards being ripped out of the ground. Why so? Well, quite simply, there is an over-supply of tannin-rich apples. Let's look at why.

In the wake of the Magner's Effect huge swathes of bush orchards were planted under contract by local farmers at the behest of bigger cider makers who, on the evidence of the summer of 2006, were going to need considerably more apples to satisfy the increasing demand. Consumers are somewhat fickle, however, so just as these extra few thousand acres of fine, tannic apples came to fruition, the demand for 'apple' cider started to wane with the proliferation of flavoured ciders. The majority of mainstream flavoured ciders will be using AJC from dessert apples grown in the warmer climes of Italy, Turkey or France. In some instances, however, larger makers are beginning to plant, and use, dessert apples varieties, such as Worcester Pearmain and Jonagold, for their flavoured cider base blend.

Today that leaves us with the spectre of numerous bush orchards being grubbed up. It's really quite a traumatic sight, but it's a more complex issue than simply being able to put the blame at the doorstep of flavoured ciders.

The majority of land upon which orchards are being destroyed today was, 30–40 years ago, planted with potatoes or wheat. In the vast majority of cases contracts have come to their end, or the grower has received a few quid to end their contract early, and the land can be turned back to growing something more profitable than tannic apples. In fact, there are probably as many tannic-apple bush orchards in the ground today as there were in the days before the Magner's Effect, with the planting and grubbing of orchards being undertaken in equal measure over that time.

These bush orchards, relative to monocultures of wheat or maize, have a higher aesthetic appeal (in my opinion), greater levels biodiversity and benefit the soil by being till free. But they do remain intensively managed landscapes, part of the industrialised agricultural system. What is heartbreaking, and one might consider culturally reprehensible, is when fruit from traditional, standard orchards is jettisoned because they do not provide the requisite desired yield. These orchards, beyond the fruit they provide, are havens for wildlife and are classed as a Priority Habitat under the UK Biodiversity Action Plan (UK BAP). They are edifying totems of the agricultural customs of the South and West of England.

Now, I know larger cider makers aren't charities, but any maker that extols the virtues of their long-standing heritage, continued family ownership, custodianship of the local landscape and the quality of product, should, I believe, extend their cultural largesse to the conservation of these highly valuable, traditional landscapes, even if it is just for the PR benefit.

Pear

I told you the fermented pear wouldn't be forgotten! Although, to look at the chart on page 80 one could be forgiven for thinking it already is somewhat forgotten by most drinkers, and increasingly being lost into the mists of time. Even more reason, therefore, for me to cogitate upon the nature, role and merit of perry in this modern age of drinks.

Before we go any further, let's address the pear-shaped elephant in the room – pear cider. For some folks, this phrase elicits a visceral response, full of bile and rage. In 2007 a review of the NACM's Code of Practice included an amendment to include the term pear cider as a synonym for perry. As *the* authority on cider and perry, as far as government legislation and duty is concerned, the NACM's endorsement of the phrase has ensured it is enshrined within HMRC Notice 162 and is deemed by Trading Standards to be an appropriate 'name of the food'.

The reason for this change was the emergence of a mini-trend in the immediate post-Magner's era of brands using the term pear

cider, and receiving a favourable response amongst consumers. Brands like Kopparberg and Brothers drove their liquids using the pear cider *nom de plume*, with no connotations of old fashionedness that might have come with perry. Pear cider was young, vibrant, different and here to stay.

For many people, the concept of pear cider is anathema: cider is made from apples and perry is made from pears. If something has the word cider on it, then it needs to have a fermented apple base. Others take a different stance, insisting that perry must be made from perry pear varieties such as Hendre Huffcap, Thorn or Oldfield, and that drinks produced from the fermentation of dessert pear varieties, such as Commice or Concorde, are not the same drink, or even in the same league. For the purposes of ease, however, I will refer to all fermented pear drinks hereafter as perry.

So, how does perry look today? If truth be told, it isn't in the rudest of health. The UK's largest brand by volume is Lambrini, a drink synonymous with 16-year-old birthday parties, bad hairstyles, angst and singing too loudly to Savage Garden (or was that just me?). I wonder what proportion of Lambrini drinkers know that it is, in fact, a perry, or whether their focus is on the sweetness, mid-level of booze and ease of drinking? Even Lambrini's parent company, Halewood International, describes the drink on their website as being an RTD rather than a perry.

What a sad demise for a most special of drinks, one bursting with mystique and élan. The traditional drink never reached the volume or popularity of cider due to a range of factors, including the challenge of harvesting variously super squishy or rock hard fruit, the natural ease of acetification and the potentially diarrhoea-inducing capacity of the inherent unfermentable sugar, sorbitol.

Just to round things off, I would like to share with you this little quote: 'Although Perry, the wine of pears, or "pear cider", is known to but a few nowadays, it is a beverage that has long been known and appreciated, and justly so.'

This description of a loved, nearly-lost, magical and maybe slightly confused drink could have been written today. In fact, it was written by Dr Herbert Durham, eminent perry expert and Bulmers' chief production manager, for the Woolhope Naturalist's Field Club in 1923. Some things never change.

Fruit flavoured

One could describe flavoured ciders as the saviours of the category, gobbling up the volume lost from 'apple' ciders, as drinkers turned away in droves on the rebound from the Magner's Effect. Contrarily, some might say that these drinks actively engineered the demise of 'apple', and the desire for tannic apples as previously mentioned. What is certain is that flavoured ciders have undergone an almost inexorable rise over the last 15 years, growing from barely 1% of volume sales back in 2006 to over 35% today, and firmly entrenched into both the off-trade and on-trade. The UK's second biggest selling pint is Strongbow Dark Fruit, while three flavoured brands

Damsons destined for
Dabinett and friends

sit in the top five most popular in retail. The volume and value of this sector is huge and is here to stay.

Almost every cider maker of full commercial viability will be creating a flavoured cider as part of their portfolio to service this demand, even if it is not part of their core ideology or desire. One smaller maker, on the condition of anonymity, stated: 'For commercial purposes we also do a couple of fruit ciders but the less said about those the better – they are annoyingly popular!'

As I described in the opening chapter, I am a man of the world of cider, a pragmatist, as well a consumer in my own right, and I truly believe flavoured ciders have their part to play in modern British cider. The also had a part to play in 'ye olde British cyder', too. From Ralph Austen's 1657 *A Treatise of Fruit Trees* we learn that cherry juice was added to cider. And from John Worlidge's 1678 polemic, *Vinetum Britannicum*, it states that the addition of the juice of many berries to cider is advocated, including currants, raspberries, mulberries, blackberries and elderberries.

There are two fundamental challenges with flavoured cider in Britain today. The first is that because they are not recognised as a cider for tax purposes, the duty rate for such drinks is considerably greater than conventional cider. A quick look on the shelves or online at any kind of flavoured cider shows shows them all, almost without exception, sitting at 4% ABV – the upper threshold before a big hike in duty is applied. This only serves to encourage dilution, reducing intensity of juice content and flavour.

The second is that they often just get lumped in together. The additions of Pinot Noir skins, hops, honey, elderflowers, nettles and blackberries to cider have made some of the most interesting, and downright tasty ciders of the last five years. However, for most consumers, flavoured ciders have a very specific connotation – what I describe as being alcopops-by-proxy (ABP).

These ABPs have no intention of placing the apple at the centre of the appeal. They tend to be entirely devoid of fermented characters, demonstrate hyper-addition of aromas, and contain enough sugar to sink a battleship, with all the associated health risks.

※

So, there you have it. Cider, understood. Well, cider lumped into boxes, at least. The majority of British cider, by volume standards at least, is well documented, analysed and understood. Now let's take a peek at what is happening within the sector of cider that doesn't get written about in *The Grocer* and doesn't get covered by IRI, Nielsen or CGA data. What follows is a quantitative, but mostly qualitative, exploration of observations, trends, themes, categories, terminology, ideologies, opportunities and challenges at the crafted end of the cider spectrum.

CHANGES, THEMES AND OPPORTUNITIES

Consumers

Cider has always had a dedicated following, whether it be those who desire something crisp and fresh or sweet and fruity, those who were weaned on the fermented apple and need look no further, or those who don't like the taste of beer but don't want to sip wine. The stark fact remains, though, that **most people never drink cider**.

Maybe only Chardonnay (nice one, California) has an equally undeserved reputation in the booze world. For cider to never even be considered as an option severely limits the number of consumers that can be tapped into, but change is afoot.

The younger generations have wildly different approaches to drinking than their forebears. These are the aforementioned curious consumers and their promiscuous palate has been largely driven through the interminable permutations that can be achieved in craft beer, but who are no longer satisfied by the latest interpretations of DDH Imperial Coffee Milkshake Stouts.

The number of platforms available to cider to reach new consumers, young and old, has begun to increase, too. Jancis Robinson MW, one of the most famous and respected of global wine authorities, has given space on her website for advocacy of cider to subscribers. 'It's important that young people are catered for. As a journalist, I'm always wanting to keep up with the trends. I'm terribly conscious

that my nice, comfortable world of growing wine is over and it seems sensible to have small insurance against this.'

Rachel Hendry from Burum Collective, has very neatly coined the phrase 'compound drinking' to encapsulate this emergence of drinkers with a considerably greater knowledge and repertoire of, and openness to, a whole range of drinks, that, wonderfully, very much includes cider.

Cider Descriptors

For decades, particular descriptors have been attached to all drinks, including cider, by a combination of consumers, the drinks trade and cider makers themselves, to help everyone gain a greater understanding of the values and essence of a drink, if not informing exactly what has gone into the making of it, or how it tastes. Let's have a look at some of the classics.

Farmhouse, traditional and scrumpy

From the smaller cider maker's perspective, and given cider's rural and heritage roots, farmhouse and traditional have been mainstays for generations. For any producer whose primary endeavour is to advocate tradition then these terms are still the best representation of that, and I would wager the consumer would understand what they're getting into. Some makers prefer to advocate the craftsmanship that comes with the making of their cider (artisan or small batch), whereas others, raging against the perceived fakeness of mainstream, industrial ciders, might use proper.

Although, personally, I am less of a fan of the term scrumpy, for connotations of lumpy bits, vinegar, and falling-over levels of potency, it's not for me to dictate how a cider maker wishes to champion their wares. There's no doubting that scrumpy, or rough

cider as it is also known, was an integral part of the heritage, custom and agricultural cycle of the West Country, and in some quarters, still is. I have no desire to deny such cultural totems – these are places and products that need to be conserved, even if some of them are best used in a vinaigrette.

As cider begins to be produced by people in rural areas who do not have a tie to a farm, who want to exert some modicum of stabilisation in the process, who are heavily influenced by other drinks or who are based in urban areas, these descriptors will hold less value for them. This conjures up the spectre of a whole raft of other terms that are used by cider makers bigger and smaller across these isles to best portray their ciders in one snappy soundbite.

WHAT'S IN A NAME?

Not every cider maker even uses the word cider to describe their products, instead using *cyder*. There is much conjecture as to whether there was any significant difference between drinks bearing these marginally different names. The dictionary will tell you that *cyder* is simply an archaic alternative spelling to cider. Given that, to the ear, the two versions sound identical, and that by 1800, 40% of men and 60% of women still were illiterate, it gives rise to the conclusion that cyder and cider refer to the identical drink and the identical process.

Others attest that these were different drinks, with cyder the finest that could be made – a drink for the nobility and royalty in the 17th and 18th centuries. There is a handful who keep the cyder flame burning today, such as Minchew's Cyder and Perry in Gloucestershire, Venton's Cyder in Devon and Starvecrow Cyder from East Sussex. According to Mark Venton, 'The only potential downside to using the term *cyder* is that it sometimes struggles to appear on Google searches!'

Natural

Though rarely seen on the actual label, a number of cider makers and advocates have started adopting certain terms from the increasingly popular Natural Wine movement into their lexicon, including the descriptor Natural Cider. In wine, this phrase pertains to a range of possible attributes that differentiate it from conventional wine, such as being made from organically grown grapes or spray-free grapes, utilising wild yeasts, or where no sulphites or fining agents have been added.

The term natural is a bugbear for some people who state that cider (or wine for that matter) simply can't be called natural because its existence, including the development of apple varieties and orchards, are all anthropogenic in origin. For those that use, and (increasingly) understand the term natural, however, it is known to pertain to a drink that is the opposite of conventional or mainstream. Sitting alongside natural as a descriptor is minimal intervention – again, to indicate the paucity of additions, and with fermentation, carbonation and stabilisation achieved through the guidance of nature.

Real

Some makers and organisations have plumped for the term real to best evoke the ethos and nature of their ciders. This, of course, is the term that CAMRA has championed for decades, aligning to its real ale definition. Over the years, the abridged definition (see page 51) has grown to cover ten bullet points across two sections – not the snappiest structure to easily convey to the trade and/or consumers.

However, in a bid to reflect the plethora of changes that have occurred in drinks production and consumption over the last 20 years and to address some of the inherent differences in *brewing* cask-conditioned ale and *making* real cider, CAMRA has recently launched its new definition of Real Cider and Perry. It now reads:

CAMRA defines real Cider or Perry as being fermented from the whole juice of fresh pressed apples or pears, without the use of concentrated or chaptalised juices.

The central tenet of this definition is precisely as it always was – to champion, celebrate and campaign for ciders made with integrity, care and apples at the core (pardon the pun), and that provides a differentiation to those ciders coming from macro producers.

This revised definition keeps things simpler than the previous definition, devoid of the multiple stipulations and available in one neat soundbite. Instead of the prescriptive nature of the original definition, the revised version then offers a number of pointers to *best practice*, including: the use of high juice content, providing as much information as possible about the fruit and processes used, the provision of *naturally* dry or sweet cider, the creation of naturally sparkling cider and the presentation of live cider.

Ciders that showcase these best practices will, understandably, receive the greatest prominence at festivals and pubs and be formally championed and endorsed by CAMRA as the best of what cider can be. But what this new approach affords is an exploration of processes and packaging that previously wouldn't have been allowed.

I am sure these alterations are troublesome for many CAMRA members. The 'live' nature of Real Cider and Perry, fundamental to their identity, is now no longer of requirement to be advocated at festivals and events. I for one, however, applaud the new approach and believe it will only serve to entice more people into exploring the full diversity that cider can provide.

Craft

I left the UK in 2013 to go and live in New Zealand and upon my return in 2016 quite a number of things had changed. Prior to my departure, the term craft, more so than farmhouse or traditional, had been my preferred choice in describing a small, rural (generally farm-based) cider maker. In the short time I had lived away, the term had been fully appropriated by the craft beer scene and had many new connotations.

Even if not particularly definable, it would be fair to say that arch-traditionalists such as Roger Wilkins or Denis Gwatkin don't match the ideals and ethos of how the term craft is used in the beer context, based upon contemporary aesthetics, language and attitude as much as scale, independence and the use of the finest raw materials.

Cider, being the slow-moving oil tanker that it is, is running a good few years behind beer in terms of response to market trends. Just as this smaller, contemporary cider category blossoms, one could easily say that we are now in a peak, or even post-craft world, with the term so ubiquitous and over-utilised as to possibly render it meaningless.

From a category perspective, I'm sure that craft is the term that will be used by the retail and hospitality trades to differentiate ciders from smaller and larger makers when promoting their wares to consumers. Ultimately, if the term craft on a label helps more drinkers try great ciders from passionate, dedicated and quality-focused cider makers, then how can that be a bad thing?

Fine

Another term that has emerged over the last few years is fine, which has been largely driven through the establishment in 2014 of the Fine Cider Co by Felix Nash, and his vision to present elegant, characterful, considered ciders to high-end restaurants. For Felix, fine encompasses more than simply the liquid, it encapsulates an ideology and a process: 'The makers I work with are scouts, pushing what is on the next horizon, doing things that are idiosyncratic and that are an expression of provenance, identity and sense of place.'

What has also marked the ciders that he champions is their placement into a 750ml bottle so that they emulate the aesthetics of wine so much more easily than when placed into a 500ml bottle. The first cider maker to join Felix was, naturally, Tom Oliver, from Oliver's Cider & Perry. Not only did he believe in the opportunity that cider could, and should, be presented in this way, he was sufficiently enamoured with the idea of fine cider that this is the term he uses to frame all of his packaged products.

✳

There are many who rail against the concept of 'fine', or indeed any ciders that seek a higher value perception, and higher price point than is currently achieved for the majority of ciders made in Britain. Frequently these opposers are folk who have been at the coalface for years, eking out a living making real or traditional cider.

Some actively want to keep cider cheap(er) – 'an everyman's drink', and something perfectly enjoyable and unpretentious. There is no reason, however, why classic, real/traditional/farmhouse cider and ciders with a higher value perception cannot co-exist. Looking at French wine, one can purchase a thoroughly enjoyable Côte du Rhone directly from *'Monsieur et Madame'* on the farm for as little as £1 a litre. But equally, you wouldn't then baulk at paying north of £15 for a really tasty Châteauneuf du Pape.

What most of the naysayers protest against is the use of what is perceived as 'marketing bollocks' to create an Emperor's New Clothes situation – a self-imposed deference to celebrate a cider dressed in full livery, with new-fangled words splashed all over it, with a wine-like price tag – all for the fear of appearing stupid or ill informed.

This mindset reaches its apogee when said fancy cider is not simply of average/normal quality, but is downright faulty. As someone who has been the recipient of more than one £12-plus drain pour, I empathise with these genuine concerns, but I see that as an issue with the individual producer more than anything else.

Technical descriptors

Beyond the descriptors of ideology or culture that we have just witnessed, there are many other factors for cider makers to advocate on the label – the varieties used, the importance of place, maybe even the name of a style (see Lexicon of Cider, p.147) – all of which are elements that have no agreement or definition. Some place the emphasis less on the ideology, and more on a particular part of the process:

- Pét Nat
- Bottle conditioned
- Wild fermented
- Keeved
- Unfiltered

My entirely unempirical assessment of the category over the last five years is that a considerably greater numbers of makers are using such terms to provide intrigue, differentiation and a celebration of the idiosyncrasy of the process at hand. This is demonstrative of, and a driver for, the consumer's increased curiosity. That said, the use of technical terms without full conveyance to the trade, and consumer, as to what they actually mean, can easily lead to the opportunity for confusion.

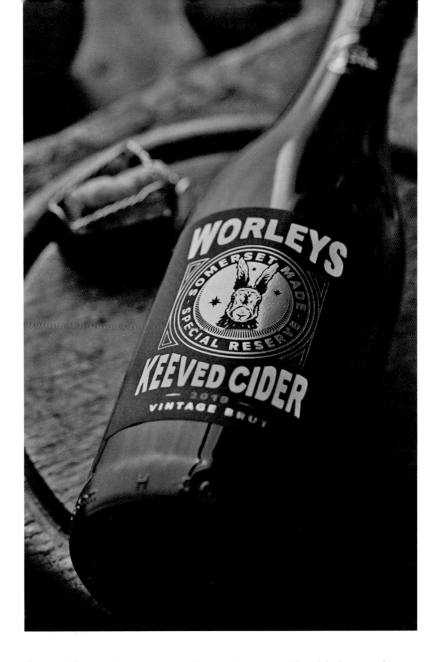

Some cider makers concern themselves considerably less with the descriptor and focus far more on the cider. This approach is perfectly encapsulated by brothers Dani and Adam Davies from Skyborry Cider & Perry when they say, 'We shy away from using labels like this. We just want people to try our cider and make their own decisions about it. It's just cider right?'

Design and Packaging

Over the years I have referred to cider as being the confluence of art, science and nature. Although my initial thinking behind this phrase pertained only to the making of cider, the more it grows and evolves, so does my understanding and appreciation of the role of art and design in engaging with consumers.

Visual aesthetics

Understandably, smaller cider makers who identify as more traditional and farmhouse showcase what is pertinent to them in their rural idyll – apples, orchards, wildlife, etc. These are integral signifiers of what cider means to them, and what they want to convey to their target consumers.

In the 1960s a number of Devon and Somerset cider makers incorporated a 'Carry On' attitude to their brands, with names such as Old Knee Knocker (not a real brand but emblematic of the approach), replete with ruddy-cheeked farmers sat on hay bales or snoozing under trees; some of which remain today. Now, I do not wish to be a killjoy, nor a denier of the culture of the great South-West holiday experience (having participated in it as an unwilling child and a very willing adult), but for many drinkers, these are old-fashioned tropes that act as a barrier to trying cider.

If the aspiration is for the cider category to grow for the benefit of all, the first key step is attracting non-cider drinkers, currently more than 50% of the British drinking population. Many of those people will have been scarred by previous experiences (possibly having drunk too much Old Knee Knocker in a field near Nempnett Thrubwell), but for those under the age of 40 the majority of ciders will not speak to them from an aesthetic point of view.

Many smaller cider makers – some newer, some older – are truly appreciating this need to tell a different story to that which is evoked by tractors and camping in the rain, or from pixelated clipart images printed off a Dot Matrix printer and Pritt-sticked wonkily onto a cider bottle. The younger, curious consumers are less interested in 'old fashioned', but they are engaged with sustainability values, keen on provenance, nerdy about apple varieties and the nuances of specific cider making processes, and favour label designs that drive an emotive response.

The key thing is that the liquid won't necessarily have to change to attract these new drinkers, just the narrative and presentation. It is this point which often causes consternation amongst some of the old guard – back to the accusations of 'marketing bollocks' hiding a mediocre cider underneath. In a small handful of instances I would agree with this sentiment, but in the main, a proliferation of bright, bold, contemporary and fun designs adorning cider cans and bottles is not only joyous, but crucial to break down preconceptions and to inspire, engage, and speak to these new drinkers.

Packaging type

The nature of the packaging of a (non-draught) cider has as great an importance as the descriptor and design in terms of conveying to the consumer what kind of experience they are going to have. Over the last 40 years, the larger cider makers have naturally favoured the cheapest packaging formats that sit with the desired mode of consumption – 440ml or 500ml cans for single serve offerings and PET bottles for multiples serves. Smaller cider makers, wishing not to invest in expensive packaging machines necessary for can and PET, plus having a desire to showcase something with a bit more value, turned to the 500ml single serve size.

My formative experiences of great cider came from drinking out of 500ml bottles. For most smaller cider makers today, the 500ml bottle is still top dog – the consumer knows and understands the offering, it is metrically close (enough) to a pint, the bottles are easily sought and a maker needs little by way of technology to undertake the packaging themselves.

The 500ml bottle is not the sole reserve of the smallest producers, with many larger makers offering a range of ciders in this format that are inclined more towards heritage and tradition. This has increasingly created an imperative for many smaller makers to play with other packaging types to drive increased value, differentiation to the big boys and to target new consumers.

This has precipitated the raft of 750ml bottled ciders in the market, as well as the emergence of canned ciders from smaller makers.

Starting with Punk IPA, cans came to the forefront of cool, contemporary and craft. Central to this was the 330ml can rather than 440ml or 500ml – a differentiator from the macro beers. This size also appealed to the craft consumer because it provided a big canvas for bright designs, didn't need a bottle opener, and was great for popping in your pocket and crushing when finished. The small volume also offered the opportunity to try something new before feeling sated.

A small but burgeoning number of makers are now placing their ciders in 330ml and (in accordance with craft beer's new preference) 440ml cans. 'Cans are fun, playful and understood by a certain type of consumer. It can be the identical liquid to what I have in my 500ml bottles, it just appeals to a different drinker, for a different, time, place and pace' says Sam Nightingale of the eponymous Kentish cider maker.

As a footnote, I suspect the can will, in the longer term, sound the death knell for the 330ml bottle, which only ever really gained a foothold of popularity in bars and restaurants.

Bag-in-Box vs keg

This heading is not intended to be confrontational. It's to understand their opportunities, their challenges and their differences. As we have already discovered, kegged cider has existed for nigh on 60 years, primarily to facilitate the replication of consuming cider like Lager – cold, fizzy and nearer to 4% ABV than 6% ABV.

A combination of ideology and cost has meant that the provision for smaller ciders looking to sell their cider to pubs has centred on the 5-gal polypin and latterly the Bag-in-Box (BIB). If a fully integrated cold supply chain system for draught 'live' cider could be created, then this could provide a fantastic way for fresh cider to be consumed in the pub. Certain individuals, such as CAMRA Cider & Perry stalwart Jon Hallam, have been making this happen for decades, ensuring the best of live cider has been available at certain pubs and at CAMRA festivals across the land. Alas, the pub trade more broadly does not have the understanding,

reverence or infrastructure to easily facilitate fresh, 'live' cider being widely available in the condition that the cider maker desires and that the drinker deserves.

The key issue here is the cellaring of the cider, or rather the wholesale lack of respect and understanding of how to cellar cider. If this were cask ale, it would be treated with the utmost reverence, passion and skill. But it's *only* cider, meaning that rather than being drawn on hand pull (with pump clip to boot) from the safe environs of the cellar, ensuring perfect serve temperature, these BIBs are frequently left to cook under the hot lights of the bar, or are in the direct firing line of the refrigeration exhaust.

It doesn't have to be this way. I am a big advocate of the BIB as a means of enabling smaller makers to easily shift larger volumes of product, and when kept and presented properly, they can provide the most fantastic, authentic drinking experience.

I am a firm believer that great cider available in kegs will be a key conduit through which smaller makers are able to appeal to new drinkers, helping them to grow their volumes and ultimately achieve true commercial viability. There's a simple fact that a huge swathe of consumers will never be willing to have a punt on a still cider, bringing preconceptions of still cider = rough cider with them to the bar. Others just love sipping, cold, fizzy drinks. By presenting a great cider in a format that is known by all drinkers and is loaded with considerably less preconception, provides such a fabulous opportunity.

The greatest advantage of cider in keg is that because of the understood packaging type, it will automatically get beer levels of respect – it will be kept in the cellar, it won't be turning to balsamic vinegar on the bar, it will taste fresh and great. A number of makers have already grasped the nettle and pursued the kegged route, such as Pulpt, Pearson's, Kentish Pip, Nightingale's, Newton Court, Saxby's, Hecks and Hogan's amongst many, many others.

Adding a different dimension to the keg opportunity is keg-conditioned cider. This process involves priming a keg of dry cider with a dose of sugar, sealing and allowing secondary ferment in the key keg. This results in a dry, naturally sparkling live cider. Strong advocates include Little Pomona and Ross-on-Wye Cider & Perry, and they believe this innovative process will help craft beer consumers view these ciders differently from the preconceived notion of mainstream kegged cider.

I know this is an exploration of modern *British* cider, but if we apply our island mentality too rigidly, then we're going to miss a trend which, I believe, is going to have a major (positive) impact on cider. As someone who has had the privilege to travel and taste sensational ciders, I can tell you there are exceptional ciders being made beyond these shores. A number of drinkers will be aware of the other 'Old World' regions — Brittany, Normandy, Asturias, Basque Country, Hessen, etc — but of great excitement, for me, is the growth in areas that are new to cider, or that had a heritage that was pretty much lost.

Some of the best ciders I have ever tasted weren't in the gnarliest recesses of the shires but in the dry-farmed valleys of Central Victoria, Australia (Daylesford Cider & Henry of Harcourt), the majesty of the Finger Lakes region of New York (Eve's and South Hill amongst many others) and in the cobbled streets of Buenos Aires, Argentina (Griffin Cider). The opportunity to try ciders from 'New World' nations is becoming a reality in the UK thanks to passionate importers of such drinks. What I see as the opportunity for these drinks is to capture the imagination of drinkers and show how diverse cider can be in terms of its packaging and language, as well as flavour profile, just like Sierra Nevada did for beer 20-odd years ago.

Urban and Rural Drinking Experiences

A handful of modern, fully cider-centric bars have begun to emerge in Britain's urban centres, though considerably fewer than in the USA. There are probably more cider bars in Portland, Oregon, alone than in the UK. Shining examples include The Cider Box in Bristol and TRAP in Walthamstow, London, and special mention should be given to specialised cider shops such as Aeble, in Anstruther, Fife, Scotland.

Thankfully, there are still a handful of traditional cider pubs to be visited. To experience famed drinking establishments such as The Orchard Inn (Bristol), Ye Olde Cider Bar (Newton Abbot, Devon), Square and Compass (Worth Matravers, Dorset) Tucker's Grave Inn (nr Norton St Philip, Somerset) and the Monkey House (Defford, Worcestershire) is a real step into our cultural drinking heritage.

There is a very small, but increasingly significant growth in the number of urban cideries – sourcing their fruit from orchards near and far, often taking donated apples and dessert apple grade outs from packhouses to make freshly pressed cider throughout the year. Notable examples are BrewDog-owned Hawkes, Luke's, Local Fox, Against The Grain and Duck Chicken (all London), as well as Temperence Street Cider (Manchester).

As Cider Brian from Chicago said at CraftCon 2021, 'meeting drinkers "where they are at" is important in terms of engaging and educating on cider. And urban cideries are important because that is where the people are at!'

As well as these in situ urban drinking experiences, a number of rural cider makers have also established their own taprooms on site at the cidery to give drinkers the full experience. This goes beyond a classic cider farm experience where one can pull up a stool with a hunk of cheddar and half pint of dry. No, I'm referring to a true bar experience, something a bit more contemporary and formal.

Dotted all over the country are makers providing such an experience, such as The Cider Tap at Rebel Root (West Sussex), Iford (Bath), Napton Cider (Warwickshire), Little Pomona (Herefordshire), Dunham Press (Cheshire) and Kentish Pip (Canterbury). These are exciting, dynamic drinking experiences, fully enforcing the sense of place and the ethos and approach to the cider making.

Innovation

Beyond strawberry and lime

For larger cider makers, the concept of innovation over the last decade has meant another blend of fruits or another iteration of something cloudy/hazy. Is this true innovation, or just continual variations on a theme? I can't help thinking that many of these so-called innovations are terribly uninspiring, lazy even. As notable cider educator Peter Mitchell told me, 'Innovation is a good thing, but it needs to be properly thought out and considered. If the drive is innovation for innovation's sake then it will fail.'

I like innovation, and it certainly fits with the current themes of exploring boundaries and expressiveness of texture, mouthfeel and experience as well as taste and aroma. Much like with my approach to flavoured ciders, if any innovative cider is fundamentally flawed in some way (whether that be through overt faultiness, tooth decaying sweetness or anything containing marshmallow) then this is not contributing to cider's cause.

Playful innovations I would point towards include Sandford Orchards' 'on leaf' fermentation and the Caledonian Cider Company's 'on branch' fermentation. The co-fermentation of fresh apple or pear juice with beer wort, grape skins, blackberries and all manner of wonderful fermentable liquids has created some cracking drinks recently, such as Oliver's (and friends') La Saison des Poire, Once Upon a Tree's Dabinett & Pinot and Crafty Nectar's #9, respectively.

The wonderful world of co-fermentation

I happen to think that the next great innovation and trend for cider is going to be dry cider. I'm not saying that dry cider is innovative from a process point of view; in fact, it's probably the antithesis of innovation – it's what cider has always been. But such is the state of affairs today that it is effectively impossible to find a truly dry cider in a supermarket or average pub. Thirty years ago Blackthorn Dry and Bulmers #7 were the last beacons of hope for commercial dry cider, but they've disappeared, too. Wouldn't it be great if consumers were aware that cider could exist with zero sugar and maximum flavour?

The perception of cider being inherently sweet irks me on several fronts. Firstly because, aside from the odd keeved or old racked exception, virtually every cider made in the world will start its life bone dry. Yes, sugar is then added back post-fermentation to the majority of products, but the quantity can vary massively and on that spectrum can include no sugar.

My second bugbear is that the **cider = sweet = bad** myth is perpetuated by respected websites such as www.drinkaware. co.uk, which inform people of their alcoholic and calorific intake. This website states that an 'average' pint of cider at 4.5% ABV equates to 216 calories. Based on that, a bone-dry 6% ABV cider is 188 calories, while a 4% Scandinavian alcopop-by-proxy could have as many as 330 calories per pint!

My takeaways from this are thus: the lumping of the calorific content of all ciders into one box is clunky at best, and downright erroneous; even a bone-dry cider contains a decent number of empty calories and should be consumed responsibly; stay away from the fizzy Nordic Ribena if you don't want dentures by the time you're 40.

Cider with food

Cider is clearly not touted as being a great accompaniment, like wine, but it should be, and the data says this is changing. The WCR 2020 points to 19% of at-home drinking occasions being undertaken with a formal meal. There isn't any particular style, flavour of type of cider that works best for matching, but those products that present themselves in a 750ml bottle provide a nod towards being treated, and thought of, as a substitute for wine.

Drinking cider with food doesn't need to be something undertaken on a special occasion only, nor should it be viewed as something elitist. It should simply be treated as part of any dining experience, heightening the occasion, just like wine does.

Cider has all of the requisite sensory characters shared with wine and, for me, is often a better match. This goes way beyond slurping a giant tannic cider with a lump of aged cheddar – not that that's a bad thing. The most fundamental thing to realise is

that there should be no rules when it comes to paring up ciders and food. If you think the experience of the cider and/or the food has been enhanced as a result of matching experience, then it has been a success.

Some direction does exist for those who are less certain about how to approach this brave new world, and to save your taste buds from a potentially challenging assault, there are four guiding principles to a successful match:

Cut/Cleanse – use acidity to cut through richness, fattiness and sweetness, or use acidity, astringency or carbonation to scour the palate and reset it.

Complement – use ciders that accentuate similar flavours: fresh acid, herbaceous, savour or spicy.

Coordinate – use ciders that match the intensity, weight and texture of the matched food so that one is not overwhelmed by the other.

Contrast – use ciders that differ in flavour and mouthfeel from the food to create balance and enhancement.

Low/No

The concept of low- and no-alcohol beverages is not something new. For the last 20-plus years the likes of Beck's Blue, Kaliber and Stowford Press LA have sat on the bottom shelf of the pub fridge, waiting to (unsatisfactorily) sate the taste buds of a designated driver.

But with the advent of Gen Z coming of legal drinking age, they have brought with them their considerable levels of self-care, awareness and self-control. They go out far less than Gen X, or above, did at their age (or still do). They are far more likely to drink at home, being more conservative with their cash, but also facilitating increased time spent on technologically based socialising and entertaining.

But the number of people wishing to lower their alcohol intake isn't solely limited to this demographic. There are a multitude of different reasons why someone doesn't drink, which could include, but is not limited to, improving physical health and mental health, weight control, addressing addiction or for financial reasons. What is unacceptable, and sadly all too frequent, is for that person to be questioned as to why they have opted for a soft drink, a mocktail, a low-alcohol cider or beer, or simply a glass of water.

The desire for drinks that provide the taste and social sensation of booze, but without the higher levels of alcohol, has become so strong over the last three years that it has created its own category – Low/No. This has been driven by beer, which, thanks to the nature of the brewing process and the raw materials used, is able to achieve drinks of outstanding flavour intensity, structure and balance, even at 0% alcohol content.

This has now well and truly crossed over to cider. In the year up to 6 September 2020 the number of no- and low-alcohol cider buyers increased by 25.7%, with the category now worth £20.7m, up 23.1% compared to the previous year. Beyond two expensive process to physically remove alcohol from a cider, most low-alcohol ciders are achieved through a dilution methodology, meaning they normally sit between 0.5% ABV and 1% ABV.

The original low(er)-alcohol cider was called Ciderkin and was made by re-wetting pomace from the first pressing which, owing to the inefficient pre-20th century hand screw presses, still contained plenty of sugar. The 'second pressing' would yield sufficient sugar to a 'small' cider, sitting at 3–4% ABV. There are today only a handful of exponents of this otherwise lost drink, one being Little Pomona in Herefordshire. Co-founder James Forbes believes more people should be making this drink. 'It has the best of all worlds – high quality ingredients, low waste, no sugar and with high crushability. It's the UK's answer to Hard Seltzer.'

Diversity and Inclusivity

There is no doubt that 2020–21 will go down in the history books as the single most extraordinary period in anyone's lifetime, with the spectre of Covid-19 looming large. But also etched into our psyches will be the societal-altering consequences of the actions and demonstrations of impassioned activists in the wake of the murder of George Floyd by US Police Officers in Minneapolis on 25 May 2020.

It's fair to say that cider in Britain isn't the most diverse of communities, certainly from a production perspective. Cider is predominantly made in the South and West of England which, other than the city of Bristol, are particularly monocultural. In the 2011 census the Three Counties region, for example, which accounts for more than half of all the cider produced in Britain, was recorded as being 96.4% White. Rural living and rural crafts are less accessible to people of colour, so the challenge is to make cider a welcoming, safe space for people of all backgrounds.

Of course, diversity is not just simply an issue of race. There is no great LGBTQ+ representation within cider, but it is growing. The Burum Collective (a project established in 2020 that provides a safe space, community championing and vocal platform for under-represented voices in the drinks and hospitality community) and other fantastic advocates within the LGBTQ+ community are entering the cider fold, and, most excitingly, the Queer Brewing Project (brainchild of Beer Writer of the Year 2020 Lily Waite) is launching their first cider in 2021, in collaboration with Ross-on-Wye Cider & Perry Co.

Historically and today, the role of women in the cider industry is, like so many other industries and walks of life, poorly documented, poorly understood and under-represented. In 2019 Elizabeth Pimblett, Director of the Musuem of Cider in Hereford, commissioned an exhibition about cider women down the ages. Elizabeth explains what she found: 'Like much of everyday cider history, the role of women has been constant but largely undocumented. They are involved as drinkers throughout all the centuries, either of 18th-century fine cider, or as 19th-century female labourers being paid in cider, though many took it home for their husbands, and farmer's wives supervising this. But it is not until the 20th century and through pioneers like Jean Nowell coming along that we see women makers being recognised in their own right.'

Cider Women was established in 2019 to facilitate peer support, networking and more visibility for women, trans and non-binary people involved in cider in the UK. According to founder member Cath Potter, 'The purpose of Cider Women is about making the cider space welcoming and inclusive, which, in many ways it still isn't. You still get crappy, horrible, laddy branding and comments on social media, which we get stick for when we call out. The response can be quite vicious and upsetting, but it won't stop us. The tide is turning.'

In direct response to a sexist social media post emanating from the UK, one of the women affected, Canadian cider blogger Tas Fraser, established the internationally supported #noappleogies campaign at the end of 2020. Its aim is to tackle sexism and misogyny within the global cider community, and to highlight the work of women in cider, with great success thus far

Where does this leave cider today? In a considerably more reflective, aware and actively change-orientated space I think, and hope. Relative to wine and beer, cider in Britain is in a unique position to set the standards for what is acceptable, and what is not, at this stage of its popularity growth. And with more voices and new perspectives comes the generation of new ideas and increased growth, for the benefit of all within the cider community.

CHALLENGES FACING MODERN BRITISH CIDER

Low-Value Perception

Cider has a broader perception as a low-value drink with a low-product integrity

Minimum Juice Content

In the first chapter I spoke about the controversial nature of the 35% Minimum Juice Content (MJC) that exists within Britain, and though not a puritan by any stretch of the imagination, I really do believe that the lowly nature of this figure is an issue to the value perception of cider. Even the USA, with its dubious food standards (chlorinated chicken or hormone-injected beef anyone?), has a higher juice standard than we do, sitting at 50%.

I should firstly point out that I fervently do not believe that MJC is the ultimate arbiter of *how good* a cider is. I don't care how minimal intervention your cider is, or whether you've racked it umpteen times to retain a natural, residual sweetness; if the cider tastes like you've licked a Glastonbury Festival toilet, then, I'm sorry, that's not a good cider. I would place a cider with 70% juice content that has character, complexity, balance and is enjoyably fault free in considerably higher regard.

The fact remains, however, that cider has a depressed value perception. Three-litre PET bottles of Value White Cider bought from the convenience store and cheap multipack cans of Mainstream sourced in the supermarket do nothing to help the reputation of cider extend beyond being a relatively cheap source of alcohol. It is worth considering that until 2010 there was no MJC for cider at all, but sat at 35%, this figure is sufficiently low that it

remains the primary facilitator of cider's gross commodification, and I think it should change.

Adding water to cider is not a heinous act, *per se*. The use of water to bring down the alcohol to a slightly more sessionable level, or to take the edge off some particularly bruising tannins, is commonplace, even amongst smaller makers, and if done with care and attention helps to achieve a wonderful range and diversity of different types and styles of cider.

There are also questions of sheer market viability. Barny Butterfield, Sandford Orchards founder, memorably asked in response to a question about MJC at CraftCon 2019, 'How many people in this room rely upon making solely 100% juice cider to pay the mortgage?' Out of a room of 100 people, two hands were raised.

To be elitist and to say that cider can **only** be 100% juice is off putting and gatekeeping. Cider needs to be pragmatic rather than dogmatic, but that shouldn't stop aspiration or mean that we just shrug our shoulders when faced with a status quo that has some fundamental issues of morality and product integrity.

A dictionary definition of cider states that it is: 'An alcoholic drink made from the fermented juice of apples'. My question is: if a cider contains less than 50% fermented juice, does it really constitute a cider? If there is more water than actual fermented juice within a cider, I struggle to connect that drink with being a cider. Surely it makes sense that the primary ingredient in cider is apple juice?

This is why I am advocating for the MJC in the Britain to be raised from 35% to 50%.

Raising the MJC to this figure will have several positive impacts:

- Lead to an increase in price for the most basic of ciders – a key aspect of improving the value perception, and reputation, of this drink;

- Provide a touch more competitiveness in the marketplace for smaller producers;

- Provide a level of integrity into the liquid – one can be confident that the cider they are purchasing is guaranteed to be more apple juice than water;

- Provide a renewed demand for the several thousand acres of orchards bearing tannin-rich apples that are being currently wound down due to a lack of demand.

This proposal isn't revolutionary and I recognise this 50% figure won't go anywhere near far enough for some readers, but my intention is to simply put a considerably more robust floor underneath cider to facilitate its improvement of reputation, perception and breadth of viable products.

Just how juicy is juice?

The issue of juice content in cider actually goes one step further, because UK cider regulations have a different interpretation of what actually constitutes apple juice to anywhere else in the world.

The fairest, simplest and globally recognised quality assessment of juice is the quantity of sugar contained, expressed in a unit measurement called ° Brix. The ° Brix level in apple juice is important for cider makers because it is sugar that is the fuel for fermentation – the greater the ° Brix, the greater the potential alcohol. Depending on apple variety, terroir, geography and vintage variances, the average ° Brix of apple juice will range from 10 to 17.

In order to uphold the integrity and quality of juice being sold to consumers, and to ensure they are receiving a sufficiently 'juicy'

A hydrometer, measuring the density (and therefore sugar level) within apple juice

127

juice (i.e., to stop over dilution with water), there are thresholds set all over the world as to the minimum amount of naturally occurring sugar that should be contained within apple juice. In the USA this is 11.5° Brix, and in the EU and the UK it is 11.2° Brix, while the Codex Alimentarius (a collection of internationally adopted food standards) sets the level at 10° Brix.

However, for the purposes of making cider in Britain, under the regulations set out on HMRC Notice 162, the minimum sugar content of juice at the start of fermentation sits at **only 8.2° Brix**. This means that for the purposes of cider making, apple juice at the start of fermentation is able to contain 25% less sugar than would be allowed to be sold directly to a consumer. This low ° Brix figure is achieved through the dilution of juice pre-fermentation, normally undertaken by producers making cider from concentrate.

The reason to do this, as ever, is cost saving – why reconstitute this concentrated juice with water back down to 11.2° Brix when you can stretch that juice a little further and hit the lowest possible mark at 8.2° Brix? Sugar is needed for fermentation, but it is considerably cheaper to source extra sugar than to purchase more apple juice. This is another classic and deeply troubling example of cider's reputation and integrity being tarnished through the reduction of minimum standards in cider production.

I would like to see the minimum sugar content within apple juice prior to fermentation to be set at 10° Brix (1.040 SG).

This would ensure that the 50% MJC is backed up by a more robust definition of what juice is, aligned to minimum standards set out in the Codex Alimentarius. It comes with a historical precedent in Britain, in the form of 10° Brix (or 1.040 SG) being the minimum sugar level for juice that the original National Mark for Cider (1931) stated. Finally, it would also contribute more to the British apple growing industry (and take away a little bit less from the fermentation sugars industry, but I'm ok with that).

So, just how juicy is juice? Well, for cider in Britain, not enough, in my opinion.

Quality Control

If these first two challenges are born out of legislation, then this one sits firmly on the shoulders of the cider makers themselves. Although there have been considerable strides over the course of the last couple of decades, there are still **many** ciders in the market that are downright unpleasant.

I use the term Quality Control (QC) in reference to the enjoyment and appreciation of the cider: whether a cider contains overt faulty characteristics or not. To follow this train of thought, one could quite legitimately argue that the world's largest cider brand, Strongbow, is the epitome of cider with the highest QC standards: it uses the most advanced milling, pressing, fermentation, maturation, stabilisation and packaging technology available to ensure that it is perfectly consistent in flavour profile and fault free. That doesn't necessarily mean that I am going to be advocating this as the best of what cider can be, although, believe me, I believe Strongbow is a superior cider compared to many of its full juice contemporaries.

Quality as defined as being fault free is not something that sits in isolation to other factors in assessing how *good* a cider is, but when a cider smells of rotting cabbage it would be fair to say it's not great. Many cider makers themselves highlight faults as their primary concern with the public's perception of craft or traditional cider. Alex Simmens from Llanbethian Orchards says, 'As a customer I really dislike faults in my cider, things such as mouse or acetic acid. And if I don't like it, why would I inflict it on anyone else?'

The first step in ensuring good QC in cider, of course, begins with the producer themselves. Ensuring that a gross development of fermentation and maturation faults, such as mouse, acetic acid or disulphide characters, aren't present within their ciders is surely of paramount importance. Cider making educator Peter Mitchell, a food scientist by qualification, laments, 'I'm concerned by the trend towards "funky" ciders. There is a lack of willingness amongst many producers to appreciate the science behind cider making. Beer isn't anti science, so why should cider be? We used to have so much technical knowledge, now we're 30 or 40 years behind wine.'

There is a slight grey area around the acceptable tolerance and thresholds for certain faulty characters, which is frequently the topic of conversation in the darkest recesses of the cider web. At what point does the presence of acetic acid transfer from being in sufficiently small quantities to add complexity, to dominating and ruining a cider? Partly it is subjective – some people are very susceptible to acetic acid, others less so. One person's 'that smells funky' (broad, complex but still appealing) is another person's 'that smells pooey'.

There is also the significance of context and expectation management. If you were handed a Gueuze and told to try it you might be in for a wee bit of a shock if your appreciation of beer had previously extended to solely Lager or ales. Equally, the gently acetic nature of Asturian *sidra,* or the rich, bretty barnyard nature of Breton *cidre* might be considered faulty in other contexts.

Cider makers must also consider the stabilisation of their cider. The use of super-clean fruit, the lack of fermentable sugars, judicious use of sulphites or some form of in-bottle conditioning are used by many cider makers to great effect to create 'live', stable and fault-free ciders. These aren't always easy to achieve however, especially if a sweeter cider is desired and also when the cider is intended to be distributed through wholesalers. It is frequent, therefore, that some makers will use pasteurisation or sterile filtration to ensure that the cider remains stable.

Transparency

Cider lacks transparency and honesty on the label

Ingredients listing

We are all consumers and the primary drivers of what we purchase are based upon a set of unique, subjective criteria: what have I bought before? How much do I want to spend? Which is the healthiest? Which one is the shiniest? Which side of the bed did I get out of?

We make a series of decisions informed by our knowledge, mood and feelings. But the crucial element to this decision making process is that we are, or feel, *informed* about our decision making. Well, that we are not being deceived, at the very least. There is legislation in place that helps to protect us. The Trade Descriptions Act 1968 ensures, for example, that a Morris Minor can't be sold as a Rolls Royce or that a banana can't be sold as an orange.

Marvellous, so we've got out and out deception sorted. How about just simply being economical with the truth? Is that legal? It seems so! This is especially prominent for alcohol. Unlike almost every other foodstuff made in Britain, alcoholic beverages (currently) do not need to have any form of ingredients labelling. This is a continuing legacy of EU legislation, upheld at the behest of the European wine community which was, and still is, terrified that consumers might suddenly become aware of all of the weird and wonderful (and fish/animal/dairy based) ingredients and adjuncts that are regularly utilised in their production.

REFRESHMENT. CIDER. INGREDIENTS: WATER, APPLE JUICE (FROM CENTRATE), SUGAR, ACID: MALIC ACID, ANTIOXIDANT: SODIUM METABISULPHITE TIONAL VALUES PER 100ml: ENERGY 156 KJ/37 KCAL. FOR MORE INFORMATIO

There are certain types of food and drink that, if you consume too much, won't be great for your health in the long term – cherry cola, chocolate, cheese, charcuterie. Basically anything that begins with 'ch'. As adults, we are left to make our own decision about whether it is wise to purchase such items, but sometimes with government guidance (on-pack traffic light nutritional guidance) and even the occasional taxation intervention (Sugar Tax). But of greatest importance is the listing of ingredients on packaging.

This is crucial, for two fundamental reasons:

- It helps make decisions that are good for your life, your health and your wallet;
- It helps understand what is actually in your drink!!

With cider, as we have discovered, it can be 100% apple juice or 35% apple juice, can be made from fresh apple juice or concentrated apple juice, can be sweetened with sugar or artificial sweeteners and so on. I might have my own preferences in terms of flavour profile and style, but that is a decision based upon an informed understanding and opinion that, it would be fair to say, the majority of consumers do not have, need or want.

I do not want to state that someone should not continue to enjoy their pint of 4.5% glugging cider grabbed from the corner shop, but I do think they should be given the opportunity to know what has gone into it, because it will enable them to be informed about whether the contents of that cider is commensurate with their needs.

If a normal drinker of a Scandinavian flavoured cider knew there were 13 teaspoons of sugar in every bottle, then I suspect they might think twice about how many bottles to purchase. Or if a cursory glance of an ingredients list of a can of cider were to show that water, rather than apple juice, was first on the list, it might well give cause for pondering as to why that is the case.

So, where does that leave cider makers? Rapidly in a position whereby they are legally going to have to list ingredients and nutritional information, I suspect. As the UK has now legally left the EU, it finds itself in a position where it could now enforce ingredients labelling for booze. Personally, I think it's only a matter of time.

Naturally, a great number of smaller makers, those with at least one limb in the traditional camp, have sensibly and proudly boasted that their products are made from 100% juice. We now have an increasing cohort of products from makers with a slightly larger scale and reach voluntarily proffering what goes into their cider, ranging from Nightingale's to Pulpt to the full suite of Heineken's brands. To see such transparency on the labels of Strongbow, Bulmer's Original et al is highly commendable and should be lauded.

The provision of nutritional information is always going to be a little tougher for cider makers who make multiple, idiosyncratic cider every years, and don't have the equipment to easily (or cheaply) know the precise nutritional value of each of their ciders. It is much easier for makers that are replicating brands with known specifications.

I am not going to be puritanical and say that an ingredients list and nutritional information *has* to be on labels. For many producers, the visual, aesthetic appeal of packaging design is paramount. An easily found (i.e., not tucked away in the tiniest crevice at the bottom of the page) link on a web page could suffice.

Ultimately, my call to cider makers is to get ahead of the game and prepare for what, I believe inevitably, will be a legal requirement sooner rather than later. Be open, be honest, be transparent. Tell your story, describe your process (accurately) and let the consumer decide if it resonates with them.

Misleading language

If the obfuscation of factual information about what is contained within a cider makes things tricky for the consumer to make an informed choice, then this is doubly compounded when a cider maker utilises language or statements that diverge from reality.

I'm not talking about terms like real, craft or traditional – the preferred choice of descriptor is entirely up to the producer, and should be done as a freedom of expressing what the cider encapsulates. But it is crucial to ensure they do so in a non-misleading way. In fact, not only should there be a moral imperative to not mislead the consumer, but there is actually a legal imperative, too. Regulation (EU) No 1169/2011 is the piece of legislation that the UK operated under from 2011 until the completion of the Brexit transition at the end of 2020 (and a proxy of which is currently in force). It states that on-product information should not mislead the consumer with regards to what is contained within, how it was made, and whether any special processes have been undertaken in its creation. Despite the clarity and certainty of this legislation, there are many products available in the UK market that push things to the edge. Let's have a look at a couple.

'Made with 100% fresh pressed apples'

The intended interpretation is that this cider is made solely from 100% fresh pressed apples. But what this actually means is: 'of the apple juice that is contained within this cider, 100% of it is made from fresh pressed apples – i.e., not made from apple juice concentrate.'

Trading Standards officials have indicated to me that, by the letter of the law, there is no case to answer here. But I can't help feeling that the Average Jo on the street is going to see that and come to the justifiable conclusion that this cider is made from 100% apple juice. Not only is this incorrect, but it also appropriates the precise USP that many smaller cider makers hang their hat on, and devalues it.

Sweet Sparkling Rosé Cider – 'made with a blend of naturally sweet, rosy-red dessert apples'.

The intended interpretation is 'this cider is pink because it is made with red apples and the cider is sweet because these apples have a naturally high sugar content.' But what it actually means is 'we want the consumers to think that the sweetness and colour come naturally from the apples, but actually, the sweetness is derived from sugar added post-fermentation and the rosiness achieved through the addition of a colouring called anthocyanin (E163)'.

I've got no problems with rosé, in fact I'm quite into the concept and now refer to it as its own style (see page 166). Regardless of your opinions of rosé, the task at hand here is to improve consumer confidence and understanding in cider makers and the cider-making process, and as such, I have serious truck with this statement. The consumer is being hoodwinked into making a fair assumption that the sweetness and rosiness of this cider is directly attributed to the constituents of sweet, rosy apples. This is fundamentally not the case.

Firstly, to a greater or lesser extent, all apples are naturally sweet. Secondly, the natural sugars within these, or indeed any, apples used in cider making are the fuel for fermentation, and will therefore not be present in the resulting cider. Bar the odd cider maker utilising clever (and tricky) residual sweetness retention techniques, every cider in the marketplace achieves sweetness in the final product through the addition of sugar, and possibly juice or artificial sweeteners. To then intimate that the rosy pinkness is derived from rosy red apples is just misleading. There's only a handful of apple varieties that can communicate colour into the cider, but they need to have a red flesh to do this, not just skin. The majority of apples that go into straw- and gold-coloured ciders are made with red apples. No, the rosiness here is achieved through the addition of one of the commissioner's permitted ingredients – anthocyanin. Although a natural pigment, what we can be certain of is that it did not derive from the apples that made this cider.

Small Maker Viability

The current legislative and market landscape does not facilitate the sustainable growth of cider makers

Cider needs a progressive duty system

We saw previously (on page 73) that the distribution of cider makers by scale in Britain contains a paucity of viable small- to mid-scale producers. Beer was not in a dissimilar place 20 years ago, and the single most important thing that facilitated the craft beer boom, and also growth of microbreweries, was the introduction of a piece of legislation that ushered in the Smaller Brewers Duty Relief (SBDR, also known as Progressive Beer Duty). This enables breweries to pay 50% of duty on the first 5,000hl of beer produced, with a tapered duty discount up to 60,000hl when the full rate kicks in. This saves breweries tens of thousands of pounds which is ploughed back into the business. The result has been a ten-fold increase in the number of brewers in the UK in less than two decades.

The 70hl duty exemption has been great for protecting small farm diversification but has also effectively acted as a glass ceiling for aspiring cider makers, preventing organic growth. I am an advocate for the introduction of a new system of Progressive Cider Duty (PCD), as per SBDR, to facilitate sustainable growth for those who wish to take their cider making enterprise to a larger scale, employ more people, use more of the redundant apples referred to earlier, and give the best of cider a viable chance in the market.

In the USA there is also a mechanism for providing tax relief for smaller cider makers on a sliding scale up 28,000hl which, if taken all the way to that maximum volume, could potentially provide an annual discount of US$105,547 (£75,000 at today's exchange rate).

I recognise that PCD could potentially put the 70hl exemption in the firing line and that there will be anger from some quarters, especially from those who are earning a decent proportion of their income from this undutied cider. One can only hope that if PCD were to be introduced (possibly imminently, as a result of the previously alluded to Alcohol Duty Review), that there remains some form of protection for these micro-makers.

Small cider representation

When it comes to matters of legislation, policy and lobbying, this is where the role of a representative body is so crucial. Cider has one, of course, the National Association of Cider Makers, which has existed under this name since 1920, and with a previous incarnation dating back to the 1890s. However, until 2018, in order to be a member one had to produce more 15,000hl, which in reality meant that only the largest could participate, with virtually no mid-scale producer between 30,000hl and 240,000hl.

The smaller makers have received representation through being members of 'affiliated organisations'. The Three Counties Cider and Perry Association (TCCPA), South West of England Cidermakers Association (SWECA) and the Welsh Perry and Cider Society (WPCS) all have information provided to them on legislative matters and are offered the opportunity to contribute their opinions on these matters, but they have no say on policy decisions.

There are frequent accusations of the NACM being a closed shop, only serving the interests of the very largest, but having been an employee, of the NACM, I can state that this simply isn't true. When there was a threat to the 70hl exemption at EU level back

in 2013, it was the NACM who fought the cause in Brussels and ensured its protection. As I write, the NACM is lobbying the Treasury for the introduction of a PCD system for smaller makers *and* the protection of the 70hl exemption.

Today, anyone can be a member, so if any maker really has an issue with their perception of the NACM, they can sign up and see for themselves. Surely it's better to effect change from the inside rather than shouting into the wind outside the castle walls?

The NACM also has an ongoing interest in furthering the knowledge of Pomology by funding a considerable number of PhD students, which benefits anyone growing apple trees. Current research includes assessing the carbon sequestration of apple trees, understanding how to combat apple replant disease, and investigating novel ways of managing tree crop fungal diseases.

What the NACM is not, and it will be the first to tell you, is a marketing organisation. It does not champion cider as a category to the trade, media or consumers. Its remit is purely lobbying and legislative in nature, protecting the interests of its members and acting as a voice for the industry.

As a result, the small-to-medium cider maker has been, and is still, grossly underrepresented. The regional affiliations are merely groups to uphold the heritage and champion the continued production of ciders and perries made in those regions. They do not exist to inform legislation. They do not have a budget for trade or consuming marketing. They are sufficiently small that they do not have the numbers to generate income, or power to wield great strength in any conversations impacting cider nationwide.

Increasingly there is a desire amongst a number of these producers to create an organisation along the lines of the Society of Independent Brewers (SIBA), acting as a champion for small-to-medium makers. But there has never been any agreement on what exactly such an organisation should have as its primary remit, or exactly what kind of cider maker should be represented.

Some say it should be based on scale, with there being an upper cap on volume to be a member. Others say there has to be a minimum juice content, but what percentage? It would be the case that 50% or 75% would be too low for many to provide a distinction from the mainstream, but 85% would be considered too restrictive by many to allow for tweaks for flavour and alcohol level.

Quality Mark Standard

Over the years many individuals and organisations have pursued a Quality Mark Standard (QMS), rather than an organisation, as the mechanism through which the best of cider could be identified and differentiated in the trade. The very first was when the Ministry of Agriculture introduced its National Mark Scheme for Cider in 1931, stipulating that a 'Classic Cider or Cyder' should be made from high, freshly pressed fruit, with no sweetener other than sugar, a maximum threshold on acetic acid content and free from preservatives and artificial colours and aromas.

Many decades later, Tom Oliver, Geoff Morris and others endeavoured to create a Guild of Craft Cider and Perry Makers in the 1990s that advocated an 85% MJC, but they could never achieve a consensus amongst the makers with whom they were conversing in the Three Counties region. Jez Howat from 146 Cider in Hampshire, along with the late, and sorely missed, Matt Veasey from Nook's Yard Cider tried to create a PGI for English Heritage Cider back in 2014–15, but were thwarted by a lack of support from the NACM and regional cider-making associations. James McIlwraith, a cider industry veteran, created the Small Independent Cider-makers Association (SICA) back in 2018 and their charter states a 90% minimum juice, but with a minimal number of members and lack of real trade, or consumer-facing clout, SICA hasn't had the impact it desired. Latterly, an alliance called Cidor is Wine has been established to provide a platform to showcase ciders and perries made with 100% fresh pressed apples and not from AJC. Its impact remains to be seen.

The greatest challenge about using juice content as the criterion of quality is that it cannot be robustly measured. In a project commissioned by the Food Standards Agency in 2004, Dr Andrew Lea assessed the viability of using potassium and sorbitol in combination as analytical markers for juice content. He concluded that, although potassium and sorbitol are fair indicators of juice content in a controlled environment, their degree of natural variation, combined with the unknown potential use of potassium sorbate, SO_2 and (high sorbitol) pear juice in any given cider, means that they could never be practicable as a legally enforceable indicator of juice content.

Sensorially, it is possible to tell the difference between 35% juice and 95% juice, but not even my olfactory and gustatory senses are good enough to pick up exactly what integer it is. Ultimately, it is a paper exercise, demonstrating how one has achieved a liquid by looking back through records with traceability.

Route to market

A long-standing issue with cider makers of small scale looking to grow their volumes is the limitation on the route to market. From a pub perspective, this is still very much a legacy of the 'beerification' of cider, with cider sales restricted to those companies that have undertaken deals with breweries and pub companies. Much like with many smaller brewers, it is the freehouses and micro-pubs that form the majority of the distribution opportunity, but competition is high and visibility of smaller cider makers to these establishments around the country is low.

How can this be addressed? Well, I think it will be a combination of the continued action of cider makers to make, present and showcase their ciders with contemporary and accessible branding and pack formats, quickly followed by something along the lines of PCD to give these aspirational makers a competitive leg up.

Identity Crisis

**Cider is a woefully misunderstood drink.
It is rife with negative preconceptions and lacks
the passionate advocacy of other food and drink**

Negative cider perceptions

In many parts of the world the heritage of cider making is slim at best or non-existent. The major challenge in these markets where cider is emerging is trying to get the consumers to understand just exactly what is cider. There is a clear understanding of what constitutes wine, beer and spirits, but trying to introduce the concept of a whole new drink can be tricky.

This is especially so in nations where the term has already been attributed to another drink entirely. In Japan, for example, the term cider is a trademarked brand of a carbonated soft drink. Even in the world's third largest market, the USA, 'cider' still resonates as 'fresh, farm pressed apple juice', appropriated from its alcoholic origins as a result of Prohibition in 1920. Even though cider has undergone a considerable renaissance over the last decade, today it accounts for less than 2% of all alcohol consumed across the country, and many people still don't really know what it is.

In Britain we have an altogether different, and dare I say, tougher challenge. For many, cider is all about overindulging at a teenage house party, or the drink of choice for those living rough on the streets. It's such a loaded and emotive term, with negative preconceptions. The challenge then is not to create a new category of drinks, or reintroduce an old fashioned term, it's about trying to change the perception of cider.

Inspiration from British cheese and Belgian beer

There is hope, however, because there are examples of traditional foods and drinks that *have* managed to find their place in the modern world. British cheese, for example, is typically a rurally produced foodstuff with strong regional associations. The unique nature of the terroir and customs of different regions where cheese is made led to the creation of idiosyncratic territorial styles of cheese – giving us the likes of Cheddar, Double Gloucester, Lancashire and Wensleydale. The requirements of large-scale food production during the Second World War disincentivised farmers from making cheese and led to the creation of 'big block cheddar' and farmhouse British cheeses had all but disappeared by the 1960s.

Spearheading the renaissance of British farmhouse cheese was Neal's Yard Dairy in London. Founded in 1979 by Randolph Hodgson, it was his passion for exploring the handful of remaining farmhouse cheesemakers that changed everything. He started working with family cheesemakers, in many cases acting as the

only outlet for their cheeses in the country. Today, Neal's Yard Dairy is a byword for cheese excellence, working with about 40 cheesemakers from around the British Isles, many of them using milk – frequently unpasteurised – from their own herds.

We could also look at the success of Belgian beer, today occupying a unique spot in the beer world as a *cause célèbre* for arch traditionalists and über modernists alike. But it wasn't always heralded. Until the 1970s, beyond those who had travelled to Belgium to taste for themselves, the understanding or preconception of Belgian beer was of being somewhat folksy and twee – one might say not overly different from bucolic Old Knee Knocker cider. The myriad beer styles weren't exported and weren't known.

The breakthrough came in the shape of famed beer writer, Michael Jackson, who chronicled Belgian Beers in his 1977 *World Guide to Beers* before his paean, *Great Beers of Belgium,* was published in 1990. Prior to this ground-breaking publication, only 20% of Belgian Beer was exported; by 1995 it had doubled, and come 2016 had jumped to an astonishing 68% of all production!

The importance of advocates

Of critical importance to the greater public's awareness, appreciation and celebration of British cheese and Belgian beer, was the role of advocates. Misunderstood industries such as these needed passionate storytellers to smash through the preconceptions, unearth the nuggets of lost joy and to be able to present these with such passion and fervour that makes people want to change habits and give something new a try. Cider desperately needs more of this right now, but we already have the beginnings. We've got consumer champions like CAMRA, brave, entrepreneurial people who believe in cider sufficiently that they sell it to the trade and/or consumers, and, of course, the all-important writers, bloggers, podcasters, educators and social media broadcasters who have blossomed over the course of the last three years.

THE LEXICON OF CIDER

The Beginning of the Conversation

So, we find ourselves at a critical juncture in the story of modern British cider. There is so much opportunity, so much energy and dynamism that it really is a joy to be part of it. But, as we have seen in the previous chapter, there still remain some considerable obstacles for cider's continued growth, understanding and appreciation, despite the best endeavours of advocates and cider makers.

For cider to be truly understood, I believe we need to give the trade and consumers the tools to be able to identify, differentiate and articulate just what makes a cider look, smell and taste as it does. It's time British cider had its own lexicon.

If you or I were to go onto the street and ask a passer-by to name a style of cider, the response would probably be: 'Sweet', 'Fruity', 'Scrumpy', 'I don't know' or most likely 'I don't like cider so move away from me, you filthy heathen, before I inflict injury upon you with the pointy end of this umbrella.'

Fundamentally, folk don't know what to expect from any given cider, because, beyond the confines of their known, preferred brand (or a general dislike for cider full stop), there is little by way of language, appreciation or understanding that exists for the multitude of different styles, types, aromas, flavours, varieties and processes that cider can showcase. This is desperately needed to give those punters on the street, and the people selling cider to them, a cohesive framework for articulating how any given cider is made, how and why it looks, smells, tastes the way it does and the words to describe those sensations.

I believe it's time to build a lexicon for cider, like there is for other drinks: specific terminology and categorisation that describes the characters, nuances and differences in the location, growing, making, serving, assessing and drinking of this beverage.

Beer and wine

A great place to start is to look at other drinks, notably wine and beer, for cider sits somewhere between the two from production and consumption points of view. Although a gross simplification, it is accurate to say that cider is made, broadly, like a wine. Firstly, in that it is *made* (rather than brewed) and secondly that it is also

Beer has well-known and understood styles

149

a fruit fermentation (of apples rather than grapes), whereby the extracted juice, naturally rich in sugars, ferments into alcohol through the action of indigenous or cultivated yeasts. This innate similarity in the process between these two drinks leads to the use of many terms shared with wine, and other terms which have been appropriated from wine.

Through the many changes within the British cider industry over the last 60 years (which we have covered throughout the book), for the average consumer, cider today is understood, presented and consumed considerably more like a beer than a wine. It would be deemed a long drink – low(er) alcohol (compared to wine), normally carbonated, presented in single serve bottles and cans and available to purchase by the pint. Viewed through this lens, much beer language is used to describe the look, feel and aesthetic of cider.

This 'made like a wine, presented like a beer' analogy is immensely useful to break preconceptions, open people's minds and to guide them to the types and kinds of ciders they might enjoy. That said, it is incumbent upon me to clarify that **cider is not wine** and **cider is not beer** – it is entirely unique.

Where does that leave us? In my opinion, in a fantastic position to begin creating a harmonised, cohesive structure to enable everyone – makers, sellers and drinkers – to better understand, articulate and advocate the full range of cider in Britain today.

The result is a combination of cider terms* and cider styles. I am at pains to point out that neither of these is definitive. I refer to them as the beginning of the conversation rather than an end. Beer and wine didn't develop their lexicon overnight, and they continue to grow and change. Also included is guidance on the common faults found in cider to enable the drinks trade to become more confident in their identification and ability to decline ciders with such faults as they are identified.

 ***See page 282 for the full list of Cider Terms**.

Cider Styles

What constitutes a style? Tim Webb, in his 3rd edition of *The World Atlas of Beer* states: 'A beer style is an informal agreement between a brewer and a consumer, expressed through a term on a label, by which the former tells the latter roughly what sort of beer they have tried to make.'

Switch the word cider for beer and this approach works for me. Although I have approached these styles with a global mindset, there are a handful of styles that are so synonymous with a particular geography, heritage and custom that they cannot, and should not, be appropriated by British makers. Specifically, I'm talking about *Sidra natural* and *Euskal* from Northern Spain, and *Apfelwein* from the Hessen region of western Germany.

British styles of cider and perry are informed by three key factors:

- Selection of apple/pear variety
- Cider making methodology
- The potential use of additional flavours

Any combination of these factors can result in a number of different styles.

Western Counties (or WestCo)

A style with its roots in the western and south-western parts of England and over the border into Monmouthshire in Wales. Made using classic, tannin-rich, bittersweet cider apple varieties to provide bold structure and intense aromas, flavours and mouthfeel. Varieties that bring some acidity (bittersharps and sharps) and fruitiness (sweets) are often classically used to provide softness and balance.

Orchards containing these varieties are now being planted across Britain, and around the globe, to replicate the overarching flavour profile of this style, but with some significant variations occurring owing to the variations in the specific terroir.

The majority of exponents of Western Counties cider are made as a blend of two or more varieties, pre and/or post-fermentation. However, today there are many exponents of single varietal Western Counties ciders that display the idiosyncratic character of the apple, which can, on occasion, be as equally as acidic as tannic.

Characteristics
Aroma: dominated, to a greater or lesser extent, by the presence
  of phenolics bringing barnyard, spicy, medicinal or earthy;
  fresh, fruity and estery aromatics may also be present.
Flavour: an interplay of tannic characters (earthy, spicy, wood,
  bitter, savoury), fruitiness (ranging from fresh to basked)
  and an acidity ranging from non-existent to intense.
Mouthfeel: tending towards increasing levels of complexity and
  chewiness with some degree of astringency and a generally
  longer finish than other styles of cider. Dryness perception
  is increased because of the mouth-drying sensations.

I have chosen to use the title Western Counties because the West Country is generally considered to **not include** large chunks of Gloucestershire, Worcestershire and particularly, Herefordshire, which all have equally as strong cultures of making cider from tannic apples as that characterised by Devon and Somerset.

Furthermore, the City of Hereford is actually further west than Bath, Bristol, Yeovil and Shepton Mallet, giving extra validity to emphasising the 'Western' nature of the ciders made in these counties.

The primary driving factor here is to provide the trade and the consumer with an easily known and understood reference for 'a cider dominated by phenolic aromas and a tannic taste profile'. That's not exactly the snappiest of titles, so Western Counties it is. I will also be advocating the shorthand version 'WestCo', and similarly 'EastCo' for Eastern Counties style (see below). Now, that is *really* going to get some people's goat and I'm fine with that. Again, the purpose it make a broader style of cider easily identifiable, known and understood as being appreciably different from other styles.

I must stress that if a cider maker wishes to use West Country rather than Western Counties, then I'm fine with that. The same goes for emphasising the individual county as well as any other descriptor, such as traditional, real or craft. The more we can give the trade and consumers to work beyond dry, medium and sweet feels like a win to me.

Finally, I recognise that not all Western Counties, or indeed Eastern Counties, ciders will be made in these locations any more, but their rooted origins and flavour profiles are so innately linked that I believe they should be perpetuated in the name for ease and continuity. A West Coast IPA is still a West Coast IPA, even if you're not in California.

Keeved

A style with a record of being produced in Britain historically, but most strongly associated with the classic cider-making culture of the Brittany and Normandy regions of Northern France. Keeved cider is, therefore, frequently also referred to as French Style. It's made using classic, tannin-rich, bittersweet cider apple varieties to provide bold structure and intense aromas, flavours and mouthfeel. Varieties that bring some acidity (bittersharps and sharps) and fruitiness (sweets) are often classically used to provide softness and balance.

The primary defining character of these ciders, beyond their phenolic and tannic characters, is undergoing a particular process prior to fermentation, known as keeving. This process involves the precipitation of pectin out of the juice, binding onto yeast and nutrients before rising to the surface. The subsequent yeast and nutrient deficient juice is then transferred to another vessel for fermentation.

Le chapeau brun (aka 'the brown hat

Fermentation tends to be slow and incomplete, normally leading to a lower alcohol content and retention of residual sweetness. These ciders are often presented in a 750ml bottle, with a degree of natural carbonation.

Characteristics

Aroma: phenolic characters dominate, often with spicy, earthy and barnyard dominating; also the presence of 'juicy' fruit aromas.

Flavour: rich, roasted, spicy fruitiness interplays with soft bitterness and earthiness, with generally no/low level of acidity.

Mouthfeel: tending towards increasing levels of complexity and chewiness with some degree of astringency and a generally longer finish than other styles of cider. Dryness perception is counteracted by intense, smooth juiciness.

Eastern Counties (or EastCo)

A style of cider that is characterised by the relative absence of tannin, and by the predominance of acidity, fruitiness and freshness, achieved through the use of dessert and culinary apples. This broader style of cider has the greatest geographical spread, being made all over the world, from Washington DC to Wellington, NZ. The name Eastern Counties has particular relevance in Britain, but also goes under other names elsewhere in the world, often referred to as modern, New World, sharp, fresh or clean.

This style is most closely associated with the eastern and south-eastern parts of England, famed for their eating and cooking apples, and also where the growing and use of tannic apples for cider did not root itself historically.

The growing of these apples, and the making of this style of cider, is not limited to the East and South-East of England. Indeed, it is made all across the UK, from Cornwall to Caithness, and everywhere in between. Depending on the specific variety of apple (and process) used, these ciders can present themselves as being dominated more by crisp acidity, soft fruitiness or aromatic minerality.

Characteristics

Aroma: fresh citrus, zingy green apple, baked apple strudel, floral, estery.

Flavour: crisp, fresh or sour acidity, with fruitiness and/or sweetness to balance, sometimes with minerality.

Mouthfeel: light and vibrant on the palette with a generally short(ish) finish.

Classic Perry

Made using specific, traditional perry pear varieties typical to Herefordshire, Gloucestershire, Worcestershire and Monmouthshire, as well as Northern France and Central Europe. Grown for the sole purpose of making perry for centuries, they are differentiated from dessert pears by the presence of tannin, providing a varying degree of boldness and astringency. Depending upon the variety, there will also be varying degrees of fresh acidity and rich fruitiness.

Generally lighter in weight than tannic ciders, florality, fruitiness and texture exemplify these drinks. The presence of citric acid ensures floral characters such as elderflower and jasmine, as well as tropical fruits such as grapefruit, pineapple and watermelon can be achieved.

Pears contain sorbitol, an unfermentable sugar, ensuring perry retains, to a greater or lesser degree, a natural sweetness. The citric acid component can convert to ethyl acetate under anaerobic conditions, leading to the frequent presence of these characters, which can be pleasant in lower, balanced proportions.

Characteristics

Aroma: estery, floral and perfumed, with potentially some phenolic and ethyl acetate characters expected.

Flavour: with a backbone of fruitiness – tropical/stonefruit/pipfruit – and acidity ranging from light to zingy, normally accompanied by some creamy sweetness.

Mouthfeel: generally light to medium intensity, but can be very astringent and bold depending upon the nature and level of tannin in each variety.

New World Perry

Made using dessert and culinary pears, these drinks have no great heritage or tradition, and their production is a relatively recent phenomenon, predominantly in the South-East of England. The drinks made from these pears do not display the tannic or acid characters of the Classic Perry. These drinks can, and are, being made all over the world, but especially in areas where perry pears do not exist.

Lighter in weight than cider, modern perries are dominated by florality and fruitiness. As with perry pears, the fruit contains sorbitol, an unfermentable sugar, ensuring the drinks retain a natural sweetness.

Often referred to as 'pear cider', a modern term created to introduce the concept of a fermented pear drink to new consumers, this acts as a point of differentiation of Classic Perry.

Characteristics

Aroma: highly, floral and perfumed; no phenolics expected.
Flavour: rich, unctuous fruity creaminess resulting from
  higher quantities of sorbitol and low levels of acidity.
Mouthfeel: mouth filling, potentially cloyingly soft textured
  with short(ish) finish.

Flavoured (Fruit)

Made with a Western Counties or Eastern Counties base cider, this style includes the addition of fruits other than apples/pears, and potentially the flowers and honey from plants and trees to create a whole new experience. This could include, but is not limited to: strawberry, blackcurrant, watermelon, elderflower, orange blossom, and other oddities such as rhubarb.

The fruits and flowers can be added at any time, but is typically post-fermentation, immediately prior to packaging. There are some ciders which are 'co-fermented' with fruits and

honey, the addition being made pre-fermentation, adding fermentable sugars and contributing towards the taste and aroma of the resultant finished drink (see co-fermentation).

Characteristics

Aroma: relevant cider aromas (phenolic and/or fruity) from the respective base cider style, combined with the attributes of the relevant fruits and/or flowers.

Flavour: cider characteristics (tannic, fresh, fruity, etc.) from the respective base cider style are present and detectable and are enhanced/complemented by the addition of the relevant fruits and/or flowers.

Mouthfeel: can range from light and soft to full bodied, depending on the base cider style and level/type of fruit/flower addition.

Flavoured (Botanicals)

Made with a Western Counties or Eastern Counties base cider, this style includes the addition of herbs, spices and hops to create a whole new experience. This could include, but is not limited to: cardamom, cinnamon, ginger, hops, basil, etc.

The additional herbs, spices and hops can be added at any time, but is typically post-fermentation, prior to packaging. The most popular interpretations are hopped cider and mulled cider. Typically drunk over winter, especially over the Yuletide period, mulled cider is served hot with classic mulling spices, just like mulled wine.

Characteristics

Aroma: relevant cider aromas (phenolic and/or fruity) from the respective base cider style, combined with the attributes of the relevant herbs, spices or hops.

Flavour: cider characteristics (tannic, fresh, fruity, etc.) from the respective base cider style are present and detectable and are enhanced/complemented by the addition of the relevant herbs, spices or hops.

Mouthfeel: can range from light and soft to full bodied and intense, depending on the base cider style and level/type of herb, spice or hop addition.

Dry hopping in action

Riddling –
a crucial part
of the bottle
fermentation
process

Bottle-Fermented

These ciders and perries are defined by a process of secondary,
in-bottle fermentation and subsequent yeast removal – technically
known as *Methode Traditionelle*. This technique may be applied to
more tannin-driven cider and perry, but more classically to those
liquids that replicate the acid drive profiles of naturally sparkling
wines.

These liquids have completed their primary fermentation in a
vessel. They have then been placed into a bottle with the addition
of sugar (and possibly yeast) and then sealed. The cider or perry
then undergoes a secondary fermentation in the bottle, creating a
natural sparkle within. The cider or perry may be left to age at this
point, sitting on the natural yeast deposit (a process also known as
sur lie) for months or years to achieve flavour born out of the
decomposition (*autloysis*) of the yeast.

The final step is the removal of the yeast via riddling and
disgorging to ensure the cider or perry is perfectly bright and clear
and devoid of sediment. Typically, they will be presented with a
cork and wire closure, but some are presented with a crown cap.

Characteristics

Aroma: depending on the nature of the base cider or perry, will be
fruity and floral and/or phenolic characters, accentuated by
the high carbonation.

Flavour: depending on the nature of the base cider or perry, will be
fruity and fresh or exuding tannic characters; and depending
on the level of time *sur lie*, will contribute increasing levels of
bready, brioche and umami tastes.

Mouthfeel: High level of carbonation helps to clean/scour the palate
and cut through sweetness, a process which is enhanced if
there are higher levels of acidity and/or astringency.

Ice cider

This method originated in Quebec, Canada, and is a protected
style here and in some US states, such has Vermont. Made with
a base cider from tannic or acid dominant apples, these ciders
are characterised by a high level of viscosity and sweetness, and
typically a higher than average percentage alcohol compared to
most other cider styles. This is brought about through the freeze
concentration of apple juice (and therefore fermentable sugars)
and a subsequent controlled fermentation.

The freeze concentration process can take two forms:

Cryo-extraction – picking whole frozen apples which are
then pressed to extract a highly sugar-concentrated juice.

Cryo-concentration – the freezing of freshly pressed juice.
This juice is allowed to thaw and the collected run-off is
highly sugar-concentrated.

Characteristics

Aroma: rich, caramelised, roasted, floral, intense fruitiness.

Flavour: a complex mix of intense, rich sweetness, balanced
with zingy acidity, bitterness and astringency.

Mouthfeel: full bodied, oily, viscous, oily, satisfying.

Low/No

These ciders are defined by their lower than average alcohol level. They tend to be made with Western Counties or Eastern Counties styles of cider and could potentially have other flavours added. To be called a low-alcohol cider in the UK, the liquid must contain less than 1.2 % ABV and also contain other flavours.

This low level of alcohol can be achieved by:

- Diluting cider with water and/or juice;
- Stopping incipient fermentation;
- Removal of alcohol via distilling or reverse osmosis.

Characteristics

Aroma: fruitiness and fresh green apple tends to dominate as a result of juice/acid/sugar addition for dilution and mouthfeel.

Flavour: fruitiness and crisp, fresh acidity tends to dominate as a result of juice/acid/sugar addition for dilution and mouthfeel, but with potentially the presence of some light tannin.

Mouthfeel: light, lean, frequently juicy, short finish.

Co-Fermentation

A new, nascent concept for British cider makers. This style encompasses the blending of apple or pear juice, yet to begin fermentation, with another ingredient that will contribute fermentable sugars and/or colour, flavour, aroma and mouthfeel. Current exponents showcase the co-fermentation of apple or pear juice with beer wort, fruit juices (from berries and grapes), grape skins, honey and spent lees from previous beer/wine fermentations.

The juice/beer wort co-fermentation is sometimes referred to as Graff, but I'll be sticking with co-fermentation. The nature of the resultant drink, from an aromatic, taste and mouthfeel standpoint, is highly determined by the tannic and/or acid driven nature of the juice initially used and of the additional ingredient(s).

Rosé

This relatively new category of cider has emerged from the USA as a drink aimed at appealing to rosé wine drinkers – generalised as those desiring a light, floral, fruity cider, with varying degrees of sweetness. But most crucially, that the cider is pink!

This 'pinkness' may be achieved through the use of red-fleshed apples, such as Red Love, which, with careful fermentation, may be able to retain its pink colouration. The majority of rosé ciders, however, achieve their pinkness through the addition of a fruit/ vegetable to the base cider. Cranberry, raspberry, beetroot, carrot, hibiscus and apple skin extract tend to be primary ingredients that communicate the pink colour.

These ciders sit within their own style rather than that of fruit flavoured on account of their intention to introduce colour rather than flavour, and to appeal to a different consumer. This very much a style born out of consumer trends rather than a technical process, and as such, will be slightly controversial.

Characteristics

Aroma: fruity, floral and perfumed – less likely to present phenolic
characters.

Flavour: fruity, fresh with low levels of tannic characters expected.

Mouthfeel: can range from light and soft to full bodied and intense,
depending on the base cider.

Cider-based drinks

An honourable mention should go out to drinks which don't quite
fit into the cider style mould, but which owe their existence to the
fermented apple. The first instance of this would be **Apple Wine**,
which is differentiated from cider on account of the alcohol content
being greater than the accepted maximum that a cider could
naturally achieve. In Britain, this sits at 8.5% ABV, although for
certain varieties, in certain years (such as the scorching 2018),
it has been known to be greater than 9% ABV.

Apple Wines are normally achieved through deliberate
chaptalisation of the juice, but *without* dilution, achieving up to
22% ABV. Frequently they are Bottle-Fermented, or packaged to
look Bottle-Fermented and carbonated.

The second primary category of cider-based drinks are those
that either started their life as cider before being distilled, and those
that are a mix of this distilled spirit and juice. In their place of origin,
Northern France, aged cider spirits would be referred to by names
relevant to the specific place of their creation, most famously
Calvados and Lambig. When this is then blended with juice it creates
a drink known as Pommeau. In Britain, the term *cider brandy* is
not allowed to be used, apart from those producers that, since its
inception in 2011, qualify for the Somerset Cider Brandy Protected
Geographical Indication (PGI). To be fair, it's a small club. The
Somerset Cider Brandy Company fought to have the PGI recognised
and proudly wear the badge on its range of wonderful cider brandies,
as well as making fabulous Apple Eau de Vie and (my particular
favourite) Somerset Pomona – their take on a classic Pommeau.

Interpretations of Cider Styles

The joyous, and potentially challenging, fact to consider is that within any one of these styles there will be some considerable variation in the look, smell, taste and mouthfeel of the multitude of different products that sit within them. I call these the **interpretations** of a style.

These interpretations can be brought about through several different factors – some born of human decision making, some more attributable to Mother Nature.

Ideology

The first thing to consider, which is not easy to do when there is so little transparency, is that the fundamental attitude and approach that any given maker has will have a massive impact upon the cider. Although ostensibly within the same Western Counties style, it would be fair to say there was a considerable difference in the way that Thatcher's Gold, Sheppy's Vintage and Janet's Jungle Juice from West Croft look, smell, taste and feel.

The difference pertains to where all those drinks sit relative to factors including: made from concentrate vs fresh juice, chaptalised or not, overall percentage juice content. These factors will impact especially upon the cider's overarching palate weight and intensity.

Blends or Single Varieties

Every single apple is entirely unique in its flavour, properties and characteristics. Yes, we can group apples together based upon their inherent levels of tannin and acidity, but even within, for example, the bittersweet sub-group of tannic apples, there are appreciable sensory differences between Yarlington Mill, Dabinett and Somerset Redstreak.

The vast majority of ciders today, and historically, are made with blends of different apple varieties, whether they be a range of apples milled, pressed and fermented together, or the combining of different vessels post-fermentation.

Blending may be undertaken to help achieve a consistent brand – something that needs to taste as close to being the same every time it is made. It is also undertaken by many cider makers to simply achieve what they perceive as the 'best' ciders they can make, or attain a certain kind of flavour profile they desire, or help balance up, or iron out, perceived flavour inconsistencies.

Redstreak 2020
100% Juice fermented with native wild yeasts
Unfiltered, unpasteurized, no added sulphites
5.8% vol   75 cl.

WELSH M

Some cider makers, however, have a desire to showcase the innate characteristics of a Single Variety (SV). This isn't a new thing: the 17th-century aristocratic cider revolution was catalysed by the development and production of cider from one notable variety – The Herefordshire Redstreak – while more latterly we have seen the Kingston Black being heralded for its singular properties. Interestingly, both of these varieties are classified as bittersharps, apples that contain decent dollops of acidity and tannin, creating a natural balance.

Of late, there has been a trend to present SV ciders made from apples with naturally highly accentuated levels of tannin. It is not uncommon to see Foxwhelp, Chisel Jersey and Bulmer's Norman presented in their own right. For some these ciders are unbalanced and too extreme of certain characters. For others, it's the opportunity to be playful and creative. It's all about personal choice, from the maker and the consumer.

Interestingly, perry seems to have a greater association than cider with being made as an SV, historically and today. This could be down to the notoriously short harvest period for certain varieties not coinciding with that of any other variety at the maker's disposal. It could be because many of these pears contain acidity, tannin and naturally retained sweetness (sorbitol) and therefore present an inherent balance. It could also, however, be down to the notorious ability for two previously crystal-clear batches achieving the clarity of eggnog upon blending.

Yeast Selection

Another fundamental option the maker has at their disposal is the choice of yeast. The vast majority of cider made all around the world will be made using a selected yeast strain. For decades, specific, natural yeasts have been identified as having certain desired properties for wine and cider fermentation and have been isolated and propagated into a freeze-dried format available for purchase.

QUALITY OF HARRY MASTER'S & YARLINGTON MILL GIVE IT
A ROUNDED, WELL BALANCED FINISH. MADE SLOW, IN
SMALL BATCHES, USING TRADITIONAL METHODS. THAT'S IT.
NO ARTIFICIAL ADDITIVES, COLOURS, FLAVOURINGS OR
OTHER NASTY STUFF.   [IT'S PROPER CIDER]

YEAST TYPES AWRI350 & PDM

- USING THE FOLLOWING APPLES -
YARLINGTON MILL, HARRY
MASTER'S, HEREFORD REDSTREAK
AND SOMERSET REDSTREAK

A cider maker will use a selected yeast because they want to exert some semblance of control over the fermentation and/or because there is a specific character that the yeast facilitates. The main genus of yeasts that undertake most baking, brewing and fermenting around the world are called *Saccharomyces* yeasts. The most considerable volume of cider made all over the world will be undertaken with a 'Champagne'-type yeast – *Saccharomyces cerevisiae* – designed to convert fruit sugars into alcohol with minimal fuss and minimal flavour impact but with great consistency, crucial for any producer of scale.

The characteristics desired in a cider will vary from producer to producer and can also depend upon the nature of the fruit available and the type of consumer being catered for. Selected yeasts are used globally to facilitate these desired characteristics, which can range from low-sulphide production (Lalvin Sensy), to aroma enhancing (Cross Evolution and AWRI 350) to acidity reduction (Lalvin 71B) to improving mouthfeel (ICV Opale 2.0 or BioDiva).

There are, however, many cider makers who choose to eschew a selected yeast in favour of allowing a succession of wild yeasts to undertake the act of fermentation. Living all around us are a multitude of different yeast strains. Apples coming in from the orchards will carry with them a number of non-Saccharomyces yeasts, while multiple wild strains of Saccharomyces strains will set up shop in the cidery building itself, adhering themselves to the mill and press.

For many, the use of wild microflora holds nearly as much significance as the selection of apple variety. They want their ciders to be minimal intervention and/or to be representative of their place, their *terroir*. There are some who would say that wild fermented ciders are superior to those that have been fermented with a selected yeast. I would say they are simply different. Is a Flanders Style Red Ale any better than a Witbier? Is a Pét Nat, unfined and unfiltered Chilean Chacoli any better than a Cremant de Loire?

Ultimately, the selection of yeast is simply one of the tools available to the cider maker to help create variety and diversity – the joyousness of cider.

Cider maker's intention

The cider maker has a host of other tricks up their sleeve to help achieve the amazing diversity that cider can afford: what type of cider are they trying to achieve; what route to market are they accessing; and to which consumers are they trying to service demand?

This cider maker's intention can be exercised via the following:

- Young or aged – some degree of ageing may be desirable to the cider, whereas other makers may wish to showcase the youthful exuberance;
- Dry(er) or sweet(er), with the sweetness achieved through the post-fermentation addition of juice, sugar, sweetener or via a natural retention technique (keeving or cold racking);
- Still or sparkling – with the sparkle achieved via force carbonation, Charmat method, bottle conditioning (Pét Nat dry, associated with keeving or via secondary conditioning) or bottle fermenting;
- Level of clarity, from crystal clear to hazy to opaque – most mainstream consumers 'expect' cider to be brilliantly clear, with any form of haziness classically associated with something being rough or scrumpy (though New England IPA has messed up the concept that clear equals better).

Terroir

The concept of terroir is increasingly spoken of within cider circles as having a prominent impact. But just how significant is terroir for contributing towards the idiosyncrasy of final flavour profile of any given cider; and can we identify specific cider characteristics to specific regions with particular types of terroir?

Firstly, to confirm, terroir is a common term in the wine industry to describe the combined environmental factors that impact upon the characteristics and properties of a crop (in this case apples and pears), incorporating climate, soil type, underlying geology, topography and aspect.

Over time, certain areas have been favoured for cider making on account of the precociousness of the trees and the quality of the fruit, and resultant liquid, that the land provides. We can still see this today, with remnants of historical, and still fully functioning contemporary, cider making taking place around Ledbury in Herefordshire, Crediton in Devon, Marshwood Vale in Dorset, and Shepton Mallett in Somerset, as well as in many other places. The big question is: is terroir as important with cider as it is with wine? I would attest that the answer to that is **no**.

Allow me to qualify this. I subscribe 100% to the notion that Dabinett juice from the Black Isle in Scotland, the Brecon Beacons in Wales and Kingsbury Episcopi in Somerset will showcase pronounced, innate differences in average sugar content, measurable and perceived tannin (bitterness and astringency), pH and acidity, as well as appreciable aroma and flavour distinctions. I also agree that certain locations have such a perfect combination of sunshine hours, level of rainfall, soil quality and slope aspect they can create appreciably more intense, complex and downright tasty ciders and perries.

What I do not believe is possible is to be able to identify the geographical location, broader or narrower, of a cider maker based solely upon the characteristics derived from the apples, as is

frequently achieved with wine, especially from the 'old world'. *Mid-Somerset terroir*
Firstly, the concentration of flavours in wine are greater than with
apples/cider because of the lower ratio of water to esters, phenolics,
acidity, sugar and tannins. Secondly, there is too much variation
in the geology, soil and topography in the landscape to provide an
idiosyncratic sensory profile for any county, or similarly small
region. Thirdly, varieties have largely changed from being hyper-
local and regionally idiosyncratic to being planted and grown
all across these isles, losing a large degree of local identity.

Lastly, and most pertinently, cider makers, unlike wine makers,
have the legal ability, if desired, to tweak and ameliorate their cider

quite considerably with water, acids, sugars, sweeteners, colours and flavours. This leads me to the conclusion that the production techniques employed by a cider maker will have a considerably bigger impact upon the overarching sensory characteristics than the place where the fruit was grown.

It is interesting to consider, for those makers who undertake a wild fermentation, whether the house culture of microflora a) imparts greater sensory impact than location and b) whether this should be considered as part of a maker's terroir? My answer to both those questions is a resounding yes! To taste a cider predominantly of Dabinett from three of Herefordshire's finest wild fermenters is to experience the spiciness of Oliver's, the leatheriness of Gregg's Pitt and the earthiness of Ross-on-Wye Cider & Perry Co as the defining and differentiating characteristics.

Vintage

A term with a handful of differing opinions, the most common (and NACM ratified) interpretation is a cider made from a single year's harvest. The term vintage can then, and is, logically used to describe the ciders made from any given year, and potentially the sensorial differences between them owing to the human or natural variations year on year.

Some cider makers believe vintage to be a descriptor that should be attributed to a particular interpretation of cider, namely one that is intense, powerfully flavoured, often high(er) in alcohol, full bodied and that has been aged.

To add extra confusion, the term 'vintage quality' was coined by Messrs Hogg and Bull in the *Herefordshire Pomona* (1888) referring to the ability of a particular apple variety to produce complex and satisfying flavours and aromas.

For those makers who simply wish to state the year of production, they frequently use the term 'Season' to neatly sidestep any confusion.

CIDER AT THE CROSSROADS

Reflections and Projections

At this point it is worth pausing and reflecting on all that we have come across thus far on our cider voyage through time, space and place. The map is considerably more tattered, annotated and cider soaked than when we first departed, but we are substantially more enlightened for it.

What we have found is that British cider is awash with contradictions – it is in a state of flux, it is engaged in a semi-permanent, internecine struggle for its very soul, and it is exciting, fun and creative. Crucially, and wonderfully, this vast miscellany of perceptions is also attributable to the sensational diversity of styles, flavours and occasions for cider that are only now being fully realised by makers, and drinkers, alike. **I truly believe there is a cider for everyone**: from bone dry to unctuously sweet; zingy and crisp to bold and earthy; still and silky to bright and bubbly; pint to flute; pale to pink; with peanuts or pork medallions; pressed on straw or the skins of Pinot Noir grapes.

In short, we've reached a crossroads in our adventure into modern British cider, so let's pause, have a sip and contemplate what is happening and what happens next.

Reactionaries and progressives

Since the 'beerification' of cider from the 1960s, the dichotomy between 'big cider' and 'small cider' has massively diverged, creating a giant gulf between the two camps. The handful of producers in the big cider camp are primarily concerned with ensuring they can continue to make cider in the way they have become accustomed to over the last 60 years – accessible of flavour, cheaper of production and easily replicable.

Say what you want about 'big cider', but relative to the c.500 makers in the 'small cider' camp, they have their house in considerably greater order. Maybe it should come as no surprise that an industry made up of so many different producers, with different geographies, scales, backgrounds and intentions should find it difficult to harmonise.

In the 'small cider' camp is a broader range of viewpoints, principles and aspirations than ever before. Sitting in one corner is

what I refer to as the cider **reactionaries**. Within this sliver of the cider making (and drinking) community I often hear ire being directed towards ciders with 'poncey wine language', with the aforementioned 'marketing bollocks' (i.e., 750ml bottle, jazzy label, higher price point) and anything with additional flavours.

In the majority of cases I am certain this is well-intentioned resistance to change, attributable to genuinely held fears that 100% juice cider, with nothing added but time and skill, will fall into obscurity. Alas, increasingly, these actions present themselves as gatekeeping – the act of controlling, and usually limiting, access to cider. I understand the desire to preserve the reputation of this drink that is close to their heart, but there is nothing more constant, more classic, more *traditional* than change. And we are in the midst of spectactular change right now.

Enter stage left the **progressives**, a community of makers and advocates trying to break through into the hearts, minds and taste buds of curious consumers. To be progressive does not assume any particular production methodology, flavour, or style, nor is it the sole definition or descriptor that could be used for these cider makers, for they are all wildly different in their geography, background and scale.

This is about mindset – of giving cider a better reputation, more love, respect, and improved understanding amongst people

who already have cider pigeonholed as something they do not want to drink. These progressive cider makers are positively responding to, or, indeed, are the creators of, new trends in the drinks market.

Tim Webb describes this in the world of beer as being the 'concept of new authenticity' – the development and utilisation of new techniques and technology, building upon tradition, to create new, exciting products with heart, passion and quality deeply rooted.

As these vocal, social media-savvy, marketing-investing, dynamic and boundary-pushing progressive makers grow in number and influence, there is a danger of them falling into the same trap that some of the new wave of craft brewers did – to be elitist. It is imperative that these makers, and their advocates, don't form cliques, become too navel-gazing or mock tradition for the sake of it. This does nothing to enhance cider's reputation and is not conducive to upholding the belief that there is a cider for everyone – regardless of their preferred flavour profile or level of discretionary spend.

The Big Tent theory

This call for unity isn't limited solely to the smaller echelons of cider society, however. I am a believer in the Big Tent theory – that there is room for everyone underneath the canvas roof of cider. In fact there is a positive ecosystem to be gained from big and small operating in harmony.

For all my desire for there to be a more level playing field, to be greater transparency and for there to be a firmer foundation under the reputation of cider from a liquid integrity point of view, I am not inherently anti-big cider. I have worked for bigger makers over the years and know first-hand the positivity they bring: ciders that large numbers of consumers enjoy while providing investment, jobs and charitable support in predominantly poorer rural communities.

That said, I believe there is an obligation for the larger cider makers to lead the category from the front in terms of vocal and visible advocacy, continuing to contribute towards its local community, investing in its liquid to ensure it upholds minimum standards for this drink, and to undertake activities that have benefits for their brands and for cider as a whole. Just look at what happened to the British, indeed global, cider category on the back of C&C's decision to go all in and promote the heck out of Magner's back in the summer of 2006. Everybody won.

My final appeal to the bigger British makers is to **be aspirational**. I am a pragmatist, and thus I understand that the market dictates the business model for the bigger makers to be centred on high volume and low value. But, that does not preclude the opportunity for these makers to make products that showcase the full extent of what the apple can provide.

Take note of how Angry Orchard leads from the front in the USA. Yes, they are the most dominant player in the market and will make their cider accordingly, although we also know they will have to have a greater than 50% MJC because that's a legal stipulation in the USA. But they really invest into broader conversations, into supporting all scales of industry and the sharing of technical knowledge. They showcase the best of what cider can be with The Walden Cider House, their small-scale making facility in the Hudson Valley in upstate New York, creating extraordinary, multi-award winning ciders. This is obviously of great benefit to Angry Orchard, but when the largest player in the market demonstrates such aspiration, it benefits the entire category.

Cider is cider

While standing at the crossroads I come to understand cider's major drawback – it has a lack of self-esteem. This is born out of many factors, but none more so than its loss of identity. Cider has changed so drastically in such a short space of time that it has lost all sense of itself.

This is manifested in the self-limiting descriptions that makers have employed for years – dry/medium/sweet, premium, value, etc. We can see it in the way that cider's voice is only loud enough to have one keg line in the pub, rather than 12 for beer (with multiple iterations of IPA alone). It is demonstrated every time a maker thinks 'it's only cider, so why should I charge more?'

Fundamentally, cider isn't wine and cider isn't beer: **cider is cider**. Cider has a personality, culture, process and identity like no other drink. Now is the time for its voice to be truly heard and understood, to throw off the shackles of shame and to blossom into a fully grown drinks diva. Notable British wine expert Olly Smith agrees: 'I love wine, but cider is amazing. We just need to appreciate the full diversity of style and occasion. Once people respect cider makers and apple growers like wine makers and growers, cider's full potential can be realised.'

Orchards as sustainable landscapes

Cider can, and should, be louder and prouder about all of the elements that make it so unique, so special. This all starts in the orchard – that landscape of intriguing interplay between the natural and anthropic worlds.

What we must remember, of course, is that orchards are inherently unnatural places. Their entire existence is brought about through a series of considered decisions about their location, planting density, rootstock and varietal makeup. They are managed, and apples are produced using methods that have been around for hundreds, if not thousands of years. They are entirely entwined with the culture and heritage of these places and today provide socially and environmentally crucial functions. I would go so far as to say they are the most sustainable commercial landscape use we have today.

The economic benefits of orchards extend beyond that experienced by the grower, however, as these cider orchards have other positive financial impacts. In the commercial cider apple growing regions of the West and South-West of England, for example, an entire industry has been created around the growing of these apples, providing crucial jobs in rural areas.

Orchards are also hotspots for biodiversity; a result of the mosaic of habitats they encompass, including fruit trees themselves, but also scrub, hedgerows, hedgerow trees, non-fruit trees within the orchard, the orchard floor habitats, fallen dead wood and associated features such as ponds and streams. As a result, rare birds, invertebrates, mammals and amphibians all call traditional orchards home.

Of course, one cannot gloss over the fact that most modern apple orchards will be using sprays and applications to control certain invertebrates and fungi. But an orchard of any description will always be more bio-active than a patch of mono-culture arable crop, devoid of any adjoining habitat, and with a top soil that has been tilled into oblivion.

We should also consider that, like any tree, apple trees are net carbon sequestrators. Through photosynthesis they are storing up carbon dioxide that would otherwise be present within the atmosphere. That's right, in order to help combat the ravages of global warming, I propose that we should all drink more cider!

Orchards can play an important role in the general health and wellbeing of individuals and entire communities. Within urban environments, community orchards have grown in popularity over the last decade, with a genuine desire for communities to have a place to meet and rediscover the benefits and pleasures of cultivating green spaces. These green oases can provide a fantastic place for isolated, or otherwise disparate people to come together to be social, active and engaged. They promote the health benefits of fresh produce and outdoor exercise, improving wellbeing and making our cities and neighbourhoods more pleasant places to live. They also offer a hands-on approach to learning. People of all ages can learn about nature and the seasons and learn vocational skills such as pruning, harvesting and grafting.

Orchards also play an important role within their local rural communities. They are places where people go exercise, to walk the dog, to have a picnic with family, to go camping with friends, to steal a kiss. There is nothing better than sitting in an orchard during the height of blossom with good weather, good company and good cider. They are also the place of wider social gatherings – celebrations, feasts and festivals.

For many people, myself included, orchards are more than an amenity space – they are the epitome of the cultural heritage of a particular place and landscape, and their mere presence is an inherent positive contribution to society.

The future of modern British cider

So, given all that has come before and all the current dynamism, what happens next? As ever, pearls of wisdom come from the mouth of the arch cider druid, Mr Tom Oliver: 'I look at cider like I look at music – you're not going like everything. It could be that you hate trad folk music, but you love modern pop music. It doesn't mean that either of them are wrong, and it certainly doesn't mean that all music is bollocks.'

And there is a symphony happening right now. Like never before experienced in any of our lifetimes, there is a groundswell of makers, sellers, advocates and drinkers all working towards giving cider the reverence and understanding it sorely needs and categorically deserves. As one of those advocates, and as someone who has drunk, enjoyed and worked with cider for 20 years, the key observation I hold is that **now is the most exciting time for cider in the last 400 years**, since the 17th-century 'ciderists' were advocating cider as one of the finest drinks made on these shores.

There is still a long way to go, however. The excitement, the voices and the actions are still primarily within the 'cider bubble'. True change and full realisation of the cider proposition will only come when cider fully breaks through into the consciousness of consumers as something worth investigating further.

This is entirely achievable, as shown by the emergence and success of the British sparkling wine, craft beer and craft gin categories over the last three decades. They came about as a result of great liquids, beguiling packaging and stories and themes that drinkers could buy into and drive themselves. Cider, very excitingly, is in the same place that these drinks were at the beginning of their upward trajectory.

So, what happens next? What will cider look like in five, ten or twenty years' time? Well, just like beer can be Carling or Cloudwater and wine can be Blue Nun or Barolo, I believe the range, diversity and occasion of cider will come to the fore. I truly believe the trade, media, influencers, and, ultimately, drinkers will become increasingly aware of the full opportunity that cider can provide, and slowly but surely, the park-bench-consuming negative perception cycle will be substituted (if not quite fully erased) by enjoyable, explorative drinking experiences.

For this to become reality, everyone inside the Big Tent is going to need to work a little harder. From the bigger makers we need a bit more apple juice, a bit more transparency and a bit more aspiration. From the smaller makers we need higher quality control, greater belief in the value of their products and the bravery to reach new consumers through using language, styles and contemporary pack-aging and design. From government we need a leg up for smaller makers to create a sustainable and competitive marketplace. From the pubs, bars and retailers we need you to take a punt on cider.

With this combined focus, the future is bright. I foresee that people will negotiate narrow Devonshire lanes to seek out farmhouse cider makers, will begin to stop by their local taproom to taste the latest limited releases and will enjoy a cold refreshing can of classic supermarket-bought mainstream cider with a BBQ on a summer's day.

I want to see cider makers talking more about their apples and more about their process to involve and engage the drinkers and to facilitate more knowledge and nerdery. I want people to be talking about the aromas of Major like they do with Motueka hops, or speak with reverence of Russets like many do with Riesling.

Wouldn't it be great to be able to go into a pub and have three different ciders available on draught – a keg-conditioned dry WestCo, a Keeved Keg and a still SV perry on handpull? Or how about popping to the bottle store to grab a few cans of EastCo x WestCo hybrid for taking the beach, or the bottle-fermented cider for the birthday party?

This is it. This is what modern British cider is going to look like. Cider is never going to have the volume scale of beer or the value potential of wine, but what it has got is its own identity, its own tribe, its own story and the opportunity to shout loud and proud from the rooftops: I Am Cider.

Wassail!

MAKERS AND REGIONS

The Most Influential British Cider Makers Today

Before we delve into celebrating the wealth and breadth of Modern British Cider making, I first want to highlight the actions of a number of different makers which mark them out as being, in my opinion, the most *influential* cider makers in Britain today. The following makers are not who I would consider to be making the 'best' cider – that's entirely subjective and fraught with much challenge! No, those showcased are, in their own way, making outstanding contributions to the betterment of cider. They include ardent protectors of heritage and culture, envelope pushers, blue-sky progressives and clean, consistent taste providers. If cider's aspiration is to grow in volume, prestige and prominence, it is going to need leaders at all scales and in all parts of Britain. Whether it be through their liquids and/or their endeavours, these cider makers are, in their own way, leading the charge for Modern British Cider.

Oliver's Cider and Perry – the pioneer

Ocle Pychard, Herefordshire

Standout cider: Fine Cider, 330ml can, 6.3% ABV

Style: Western Counties

Notes: Resinous pine needles, and hay barn freshness abound before leaning into big orange juiciness with a playful bitterness and gentle, mouth-cleansing astringent rip.

Over the last 20-plus years Tom Oliver has made some of the most complex, and often confounding, ciders and perries in the UK, or anywhere in the world. His willingness to be experimental, to try new things, to trust other people's instincts and expertise when it comes to flavour profile, packaging and design, ensure that while also being the most traditional of cider makers, he is also the most current and contemporary. He is the ultimate collaborator, seeking out the best of fermenting talent in the USA (Ryan Burk) and UK (Jonny Mills).

The adulation that he gets from all corners of the globe is no accident. No one else has done more to be seen and heard, to be collaborative and ultimately to make cider a more respected drink. He is constantly putting his hand up, committing time, money and liquid to any activity that advances the cause of cider.

He changes minds, perceptions and taste buds. If every cider maker contributed the same amount of time and effort to the cause of cider in its absolute broadest sense, our precious drink would be considerably more greatly appreciated than it currently is.

Westons – big cider with heart

Much Marcle, Herefordshire

Standout cider: Henry Westons Vintage Perry, 7.4% ABV

Style: Classic Perry

Notes: Elderflowers and lychees and grapefruit and candyfloss and pears. All the pears.

Yes, they're big. Yes, their ciders sit less than 100% juice. Yes, their ciders have evolved over time to become more soft and accessible. But, by my calculation, Westons are the largest producer of fresh juice fermented cider in the world. To make around 40 million litres of cider a year from locally grown apples, which are then fermented for weeks and matured for months is important. It demonstrates that cider can be made on such a scale that satisfies the challenging demands of supermarkets and national pub groups, but can still be made with integrity and with a foot in the traditional camp.

They also genuinely do care about more than simply how their bottom line looks. A great example of this is Westons' dedication to continue making their Henry Westons Vintage Perry. I suspect this product accounts for less than 1% of their total volume, which would make it the victim of a SKU rationalisation at any other major cider maker. So why do Westons continue to make it? Because they know that for many of the old pear orchards, without the opportunity to sell to Westons, there is a chance these trees would lose their attractiveness or viability and might well be removed, hastening the loss of an historic cultural and landscape asset.

THE
GENERAL

Sandford Orchards – the cider realists

Crediton, Devon

Standout cider: The General 2019 Vintage, 8.4% ABV

Style: Western Counties

Notes: Claiming the crown from Henry Westons Vintage Reserve for the best of robust, high alcohol, vat aged ciders, The General is like a liquid Christmas pudding (in the best way) offering notes of seville orange, plum and baked apples before a long, warming finish.

Always beware a farmer with a philosophy degree! Barny is one of those people you'd want to be in the trenches with – he's got your back. And although, through dedication, skill, ontrepreneurialism and freakish agricultural engineering skills, his business has grown to be big(gish), his heart remains right where it always has – deep in the Devon countryside.

Sandford Orchards are at the forefront of cider makers emerging from the 'small scale' end of the spectrum and into the no man's land that is 'medium scale', so crucial for cider's visibility and continued growth. Nobody is currently doing more to make the cider-making world more democratic or viable for collective growth than Barny. He identifies young, keen and driven cider-making talent and allows them to fly free and learn their craft in the cidery without being micro-managed. Barny trusts their skills, their palates and their opinions.

Barny likes to give back to the cider community, too. In only 2003 he was a fresh-faced, eager cider maker, lusting for guidance and support, without there being too much around. So, now he's decided to play the older brother role through the Sandford Orchards Breakthrough Cider Awards, a competition aimed at supporting smaller producers' development through a cash prize plus (more crucially) technical and trade support.

Pulpt – the new-fashioned fermenters

Somerton, Somerset

Standout cider: Flare, 4.8% ABV

Style: Western Counties

Notes: Quite possibly the best nationally available cider thanks to a recent supermarket listing, this is the ultimate all-rounder. Enough phenolic character and tannic structure to appease the cider-heads and enough florality and smoothness to appeal to anyone looking for a fun, refreshing drink.

Al Collar and Jim Wakefield are on a mission to make cider more interesting for the many, not the few. The result is Pulpt. Calling upon the brightness and dynamism of craft beer, Pulpt is endeavouring to fill the gaping chasm of opportunity that still exists for cider – making high juice content, super clean, highly accessible and easily sourced ciders with eye-catching contemporary design. This is no easy task – but they're succeeding.

In the spring of 2021, their flagship brand, Flare, was listed in 529 TESCO stores. This marked the first time that an independent, British cider maker has a product on the supermarket shelves that showcases cider as a modern drink, as a drink with value, as something associated with contemporary rather than traditional. This is hugely significant because it shows the average (rather than curious) consumer, that there are interpretations of cider other than alcopops-by-proxy, white cider or classic mainstream.

It's not that they aren't proud of their Somerset roots – far from it. They use South West grown bittersweet and bittersharp apples, but crucially seek to emphasise the unique flavour characters than be achieved from these varieties, rather than an old Massey Fergusion tractor that may (or may not) have carried them.

Pulpt are also passionate about transparency, providing an ingredients list, and giving as much information as possible to the consumer about how the cider actually *tastes*. There is no dry/medium/descriptor on the front. Instead they use a concise and space saving flavour wheel on the side panel.

Only a few years into their cider journey, watch out for Pulpt continuing to make waves in the near future.

Hecks Cider – the farmhouse heritage defenders

Street, Somerset

Standout cider: Oldfield Perry SV 2020, 4.2% ABV

Style: Classic Perry

Notes: The 2019 Oldfield SV perry was one of the best perries I have ever tasted, dispelling the myth (that I perpetuate) that the best perries are grown and made within sight of May Hill in Gloucestershire. Thankfully, the 2020 vintage is equally as good as the 2019, providing limes, slate minerality, ripe peaches and grippy astringency.

Walking through the door at the Hecks Cider barn is like passing through a vortex straight back to that long distant and nearly forgotten era of pre-industrialised agriculture. The walls are coated in healthy doses of microflora, manifold barrels lurk in the darkness and there is enough cider paraphernalia, photos and old making equipment to warrant this being considered a museum. The incongruous nature of turning off a suburban road into the farmyard only heightens the experience.

The walls are also coated with a huge selection of awards and certificates for the Hecks family has a pedigree of quality cider making going back to at least 1841, and on the current site at Middle Leigh since 1896. Hecks is the finest example of farmhouse, traditional multi-generational cider making that we have in Britain today, making ciders with simplicity and care.

The Hecks family also stand out for their willingness over the years to try new things. The planting of perry pear trees in the 1990s and 2000s has subsequently led to a slew of award-winning perries, while a recent foray into naturally sparkling ciders and perries has precipitated some fabulous experiences. Tradition and progress, hand in hand.

Ross-on-Wye Cider and Perry Co –
the cider maker's cider maker

Ross-on-Wye, Herefordshire

Standout cider: Flakey Bark Perry 2017 Batch #2, 6.7% ABV

Style: Classic Perry

Notes: It's not easy to convey the myriad sensations here. Smells of passion fruit and confected bananas, tastes of smoky lapsang souchong tea, rounded off with the most supremely textural mouthfeel.

Many of the makers featured in this book who sent me ciders to taste sent their wares in a box previously housing Ross-on-Wye Cider and Perry that they had obviously devoured. They truly are the cider maker's cider maker. But what makes them so loved and revered?

It might be because Mike Johnson, along with his Father, Kenelm, were making award-winning ciders as far back as the 1980s. It might be because there has been an open-door policy at Broome Farm for decades whereby any aspiring maker is given an effective apprenticehip and is invariably sent home with copious quantities of juice with the cheery instruction to learn by doing it yourself.

It might be because Mike and his cider-making team – John, Bob and son Albert – produce a greater number of single varieties than any other cider maker on the planet (I have no actual evidence of this, but who is going to have 60-plus different bottled liquids available to purchase at any one time?). No cider maker has done more to advocate the range, and diversity of flavours produced from, the multitude of cider apple varities in existence today.

Is there a cider maker who bears the 'and Perry Co' in their title with greater pride and passion? Perry isn't an addendum to their production, it gets an equal billing of importance and is revered for the magical place it retains in this region as well as the sublime drink it can produce.

Albert's ascent to becoming the day-to-day voice and brand director has coincided with contemporary messaging and branding, as well as the launch of the UK's first Cider Club and fervent drive to champion dry, 'live' cider, making it accessible to enjoy through refining the bottle-conditioning technique as well as experimenting with keg conditioning.

Pilton Cider – the artist

Shepton Mallet, Somerset

Standout cider: In Touch 2, 5.5% ABV

Style: Co-Fermentation

Notes: Created with the help of master blender, Martyn Goodwin Sharman, this iteration of the In Touch series sees pressed Bacchus grapeskins added to keeved juice and allowed to ferment together. The result is a harmonious balance between the lightly bitter, juicy keeve and the delicate green herbeacousness of the Bacchus.

Martin Berkeley is an understated man, but you'll do well to find someone with more energy and desire to be creative and boundary pushing with their cider making without losing any heart, integrity or quality. The result is the über-progressive Pilton Cider. Based in Shepton Mallett, Pilton Cider is certainly not the first British cider maker to perfect the keeving methodology (West Milton and New Forest Cider Co, amongst many others, are particularly fine exponents), but since its launch in 2014 no other cider maker in Britain has keeving at the core of every single cider they make.

Barring, maybe, Mr Oliver, no other maker has a more collaborative mindset, either. As that concept is derived from the craft beer world, it is no surprise that Martin has worked with some of the most highly regarded, including Wild Beer, Yonder and Left Handed Giant among others. And much to the irritation of some of the classicist cider makers, Martin has had particular fun playing with other flavours. He likes to look at what he has at his disposal in his immediate vicinity, which has led him to blend and invariably co-ferment, his cider with cherries, quince, blackcurrants and hops.

Pilton
In Touch 2

If you can, keep
this cider until 6pm
Friday 23rd April and
join us then on our
@piltoncider
Instagram account
for a grand reveal
and shared first
tasting.

We'll understand if
you can't resist,
just buy another
bottle and please
don't share the
label on social
media until then.

Cheers!
Martin
Pilton Cider

I'll try to keep in touch.

a blend of naturally sweet
keeved ciders from
season 2018-2019
in contact with
Pinot noir grape skins

Pilton

Caledonian Cider Co – the boundary pusher

Black Isle, Highlands

Standout cider: Islay Cask Cider, 7% ABV

Style: Keeved

Notes: The softest of velveteen tannins combine with naturally unfermented sugars to give a big, oily, juicy mouthfeel and mango intensity. But this is neatly punctuated by the soft medicinality of the peat reek coming from the Islay casks. Magic.

Making cider closer to Norway than Newton Abbot comes with its challenges, but it doesn't stop Ryan Sealey from showcasing the quality of cider that can be made so far from cider's more celebrated heartland regions. A proud Devonian far from home, there are few makers more fanatical about their craft and their artistry, and with the desire to learn and experiment than Ryan. He acts as a proud, shining beacon for what can be achieved on the extremities of British cider geography and does so with a permanent smile on his face.

He loves cider so much that he once turned up for an interview with a maker in Somerset, having travelled 520 miles and with his worldly possessions in a rucksack, hoping they would take a punt on him. They did, and his cider tutelage began, subsequently taking in experiences in Cornwall and Brittany to boot. It's this combination of passion and playfulness that leads Ryan to make some of the most balanced, layered and complex ciders in Britain, which would happily grace the menu of any natural wine bar.

Ryan uses his northerly location to his advantage, with the cool autumnal and winter temperatures forcing slow, aroma and flavour-enhancing fermentations, while he also has prime access to the finest whisky casks for maturation.

This is cider making with a smile – Ryan's, and yours, too, once you've tasted his cider. That's about as good as it gets, right?

Little Pomona Orchard & Cidery – the terroiristes

Bromyard, Herefordshire

Standout cider: Hard Rain Quince 3.8% ABV

Style: Co-Fermentation

Notes: To quote Martyn Goodwin Sharman, it's like Lilt on the nose and into the palate the pineapple and mango continues to ooze. But of course, being a ciderkin, it reverts to super-lightness, pithy grippiness, and the cleanest of clean finishes. This shows that intensity can still be achieved at 3.8% ABV.

In the vanguard of the progressive cider makers sit James and Susanna Forbes and their exploration of cider – Little Pomona. Formerly of wine industry and drinks journalism backgrounds, respectively, they take their knowledge and passion from other drinks, but especially natural wine, and apply a playful, innovative and value-enhancing approach to their libations.

With small batch productions, a wonderfully zealous approach to cider making, engaging story telling and great marketing, Little Pomona have become the first producer in Britain to create ciders with *hype*. These are drinks that drive a fervent need for drinkers to get their hands upon, with each new release eagerly anticipated and often selling out before most people even new it existed.

Although proudly passionate about the nuance of variety, maturation vessel and time, their fermented gaze extends beyond apples and pears, incorporating hops, cherries and quince. This reaches its zenith in the form of the Hard Rain series of newly imagined, lower alcohol ciderkins.

James and Susanna are also woven into the fabric of the progressive cider community. They are simply fantastic advocates for our industry and are involved with, drive or create, pretty much EVERY endeavour that exists to give cider's reputation a jump start. If you're a member of Cider Women, have ever read Full Juice magazine or the Graftwood zine, or attended CraftCon, you can thanks these folks.

So, got get your hands of a bottle of Little Pomona today (if you can find it!).

Nightingale Cider Co – the optimists

Tenterden, Kent

Standout cider: Wild Disco, 5.5% ABV

Style: Eastern Counties

Notes: Maybe the most intensely perfumed cider in the country? Jasmine and roses pour out of the glass and it gets better in the mouth with the cleanest of acidity, oily melon and grippy nectarine sensations. Sensational.

Nobody does more than the Nightingale Cider Co to demonstrate that diversity, complexity and playfulness is not solely the domain of those using big, bold, phenolic bittersweet apples. A proud champion of the Eastern Counties cider tradition, Sam Nightingale, together with brother, Olly, uses a range of dessert and culinary apples from the family farm in Tenterden, Kent, to make fresh and floral ciders. But what sets Nightingale apart is the constant desire to improve, to do things the hard way, the relentless endeavour to be contemporary, to learn from others and to simply make the act of drinking cider a joyous experience!

Nightingale Cider Co perfectly bridges the traditional and contemporary divide, making wild ferment, full juice, often aged ciders, and yet packing and presenting them to appeal to the modern, curious consumer. An early adopter of the key keg, and pioneering the use of the 440ml can, Nightingale Cider Co makes great cider more accessible and appealing to people who wouldn't normally give it a try. This persuasion for trial is elevated by the brightest and cleanest branding of any maker in the country, thanks to acclaimed designer, and local neighbour, Anthony Burrill.

Scotland

The North

Ireland

Wales

West
Midlands

East
Midlands

The East

Herefordshire

Gloucestershire

The South

The
South-East

Somerset

South Coast

Devon

Cornwall

The Best of British Cider Making

After all this discussion of ciders and makers, we have now arrived at the point where we can highlight those who are contributing towards this age of modern British cider, each in their own unique way. I have endeavoured to select a broad range of producers here, with considerable variances in scale and ideology, whilst also wishing to showcase as many styles and interpretations as possible. Some will be niche, some will be available in the supermarkets. Some will be minimally intervened, some will be highly tweaked. Some will be still, dry, bottle-fermented, naturally sweet or anywhere in between.

This section is a celebration of the diversity of cider in every sense of the word, adhering to Big Tent principles, and championing those makers who are contributing to the betterment of modern British cider. Alas, space constraints mean I have not been able to feature every maker that I would have wished. This is both challenging and heartening for me, demonstrating the sheer number of wonderful makers we have right across Britain today.

Cornwall

One might expect cider to have a proud heritage in this most south-westerly of counties, and indeed, cider has been made here for a very long time. Haye Farm, in St Veep, near Lostwithiel, claims to have the oldest pedigree of cider making of any farm anywhere in England, with records dating back to the 13th century. Cornwall does have a number of indigenous apple varieties that were being made for cider, most famously Tommy Knights, but the flavour profile of many of these apples (light bittersharp) betrays their likely use as a multi-purpose apple – eating, cooking and cidering.

It is also the same rugged landscape that attracts hordes of tourists and second-homers, which precluded the easy and widespread growing of apples and making of cider within the county. This, combined with a scarcity of population and the sheer distance from the rest of the consuming nation, meant that cider making remained very much a small-scale affair, mostly confined to the sheltered valleys on the south coast. As such, cider never developed the depth of heritage that neighbouring Devon achieved.

Today, there are makers dotted all over the county, with several bravely disproving the theory that apple trees don't grow on the gale-hammered northern coast. Most have taken their cue from Devon, Somerset and Herefordshire in using classic, tannin-rich apples, but many frequently use the more acid driven varieties, too.

Gould Ciders & Perries

Grampound

Standout cider: Kingston Black SV Vintage 2019, 7.4% ABV

Style: Western Counties

Notes: This cider is like a teenager fleeing the nest – young, rebellious and with so much potential. It's as spicy as hell – allspice and clove – enhanced by a prickly bitterness and will be just sensational with food.

It's always exciting to find a cider maker hitherto totally unknown to you that really impresses, such as Gould did in later 2020. Husband-and-wife team Jonathan and Juliet are passionately green fingered, which led to the planting of an orchard at their property near Truro, including classic cider varieties from Somerset and Devon, some local Cornish varieties, a number of Breton varieties, and, interestingly, a number of perry pears (is there anyone else doing Cornish perry?). With this great fruity palate, they create ciders and perries across a spectrum of still, keeved, bottle-fermented SVs or blends.

St Ives Cider

St Ives

Standout cider: Kirthenwood, 5.6% ABV

Style: Western Counties

Notes: This does exactly what you want from the Taste of the West Champion Cider 2020 – it puts a smile on your face. A wonderful combination of big, nectarine juiciness, velveteen tannins and pleasing sour creaminess.

With a background in winemaking stretching back decades, David Berwick ditched it all for making cider in 2012 and he hasn't looked back since. In his own words, David's cider making ethos tends towards 'traditional with modern twists on it'. He likes to incorporate the use of classic Western Counties apple varieties such as Harry Master's Jersey, Dabinett and Kingston Black with heritage Cornish apples, and, through careful fermentation and maturation, creates ciders with cleanliness and freshness at the forefront.

Crackington Cider

Crackington Haven

Standout cider: Vintage, 8.2% ABV

Style: Western Counties

Notes: This is the epitome of how British cider can be presented and drunk like a still table wine. Perfectly branded, the cider pours a burnt gold colour and has the mahogany and leather aromas of a library at a stately home. It has the structure and composition of an orange wine – gently spicy, satisfying, neatly astringent and with a savoury finish. This is sensational. Buy this instead of any English-produced still white wine. Seriously.

Jon and Sam Miles make their cider from orchards perched on the steep slopes above Crackington Haven, a giant crevice in the North Cornish coastline. Many of the cider stalwarts are planted here, such as Dabinett, Yarlington Mill and Browns, but also a lot of Cornish varieties such as Collogett Pippin, Lord of the Isles, Tommy Knight and Manaccan Primrose. They have thus far majored on still cider although this year will see the release of a carbonated medium sweet cider as well as a bottle-fermented offering.

Haywood Farm Cider

St Mabyn

Standout cider: Original Draught, 6% ABV

Style: Western Counties

Notes: Straight from the barrels in the shop and into the jerry can like the good old days. This still, dry cider is citrusy, grassy, light and smooth, with a gentle creamy, leathery finish.

Tom Bray is one of those people you just can't help but like, with a marvellously self-deprecating humour ('I refer to my cider as craft because it's one of the descriptors I can spell'). After discovering local farm cider in his teens, he set about forming a cider society, which spawned a passion that turned into the business we find today. Tom only uses sharp and bittersweet apples grown on the farm to make fresh, clean, accessible ciders.

Healey's Cornish Cyder

Penhallow

Standout cider: Scotch Whiskey Reserve, 8.4% ABV

Style: Western Counties

Notes: Big, warm, boozy and lovely. The Scotch comes through as vanilla and honeycomb, gently massaging the fruity, spicy and nicely tannic cider beneath. A nightcap.

Cornwall's largest cider (cyder) maker was established in 1980 by David and Kay Healey, eying an opportunity to fill a niche in the Cornish tourist and drinks industries. Over 500,000 people now visit the cidery in Penhallow on an average year, sampling the range of cyders, including the legendary Cornish Rattler – the draught cyder of choice in the far South-West and beyond. Complementing their use of heavier bittersweets (which make up the majority of their barrel-aged ciders), Healey's also like to use the earlier harvesting varieties developed by the NACM and LARS in the 1980s and 1990s, as they give a brightness and 'vinous' quality to the cyders.

Devon

If there is one county in Britain today that is a shadow of its former cider glory, it must be Devon. Back in 1883 it was recorded as having 26,348 acres of land under orchard, just 717 acres fewer than Herefordshire and 2,941 acres more than Somerset, the two counties that produce the greatest quantity of cider today. Why did Devon suffer such a decline in total orcharding and cider over the years? According to James McIlwraith from Sampford Courtney Cider and the Devon Cider Makers Guild, through which much of this information is derived, it's all down to something that Devon has plenty of – rain.

As we have already seen, the 20th century saw Britain move from the small, farmhouse cider-making culture, with hundreds, probably thousands of practitioners in Devon alone, to a steadily decreasing number of larger makers – including Whiteways of Whimple. The sheer quantity of rainfall that the county receives, combined with the acidic soils and quantity of land higher than 100m above sea level makes it challenging to grow apples in the 'bush orchard' style necessary to achieve the high yield and make it economically viable to satisfy such a large maker. Devon's cider reputation was also severely impacted by Devon Colic, first described in detail by Totness MD John Huxham in 1738. Amongst a range of very unpleasant symptoms were vomiting, cold sweats, stomach cramps, paralysis and occasionally death. It took until 1767, however, for George Baker, a renowned polymath of his day, to attribute the cause of Devon Colic to lead poisoning: the use of lead for lining mills and presses was common in Devon.

Today, there are still a number of the older cider farms – Brimblecombe's, Grays, Countryman, etc. – and an emergence of makers who are exploring this virtually lost heritage. Cider making remains tough in the wet, windswept northern part of the county, with the majority of makers nestled in the lee of hills in its interior, and the sheltered valleys of the south coast. Collectively, they are all doing their part to restore this proud heritage.

Find & Foster Fine Ciders

Huxham

Standout cider: Carter, 8% ABV

Style: Bottle-Fermented Cider

Notes: Using rare varieties such as Devonshire Quarrendon, American Mother, Ellison's Orange and Cornish Pine, this demonstrates just how elegant cider can be. This cider is dominated by wet-stone minerality and salinity alongside subtle notes of pear, green apple and olive.

Possibly the standard bearers for the fine cider movement, although such is the modesty of Polly and Mat Hilton that they would never proclaim such a thing themselves. The aim of this talented young husband-and-wife team is to locate old, gnarled orchards and rare extant – especially native Devon – apple varieties (Find) and to work with farmers to help them breathe life back into traditional orchards on their farms, to prevent further decline and the extinction of important local apple varieties (Foster). The results are some of the most elegant and cleverly crafted bottle-fermented and keeved ciders available in Britain today.

Smith Hayne Orchards

Between Crediton and Tiverton

Standout cider: Vintage Special Reserve 2018, 4.5% ABV

Style: Keeved

Notes: Nostril-filling crème caramel aromas entice you in and lead to the anticipation of considerable sweetness. While the naturally retained sugars are definitely present, they are more than tempered by the zip of acidity down the side of the tongue and big, chewy, earthy tannins.

Anna and Will Chambers moved to Smith Hayne ten years ago and promptly set about using the fruit from their 12-acre, 1970s planted, ex-Taunton Cider orchard to make their own cider, as well as supply other local makers. Taught the dark arts of keeving cider making by neighbours, Anna and Will had a desire to make ciders in the *Normandoise* method that they so enjoyed. They've mastered the knack of keeving remarkably quickly, and also produce a full-bodied and fruity *methode traditionelle* cider every year.

Green Man Cider

Landkey

Standout cider: Morgan Sweet SV 2019 Vintage, 6.3% ABV

Style: Western Counties

Notes: Like many of the ciders I have tasted from North-East USA, this one is wonderfully herbaceous, full of mint and sage. A wonderful dry minerality and nectarine palate is offset by a softness and unsuspecting, but most welcome, lingering bitterness.

The Green Man story begins, as it often does, with a desire to hang out with mates and share a drink or two. For neighbours Ben Totterdell and Simon Houghton, this then graduated into buying up a former cider maker's kit, and before they knew it they were making cider to sell. For Ben, having grown up in central Somerset, where drinking a pint of rough from the farm gate was more of a rite of passage than a pleasurable experience, his focus is on ensuring the Green Man ciders are super clean and approachable, rather than all barnyard funk and leather.

Ridge & Furrow Cider

Mutterton

Standout cider: Medium, 5% ABV

Style: Western Counties

Notes: Gosh, this is a good cider. It is apple skins and apricot fruitiness rather than the phenolics that shines through on the nose, while the palate is a lesson in balance. Creamy, and juicy from the arrested fermentation, but with wiggly, lemony acidity and fabulously puckering astringency.

Named after an old orchard planted on a ridge and furrow system, Justin Bartley established his cider making on the family farm, quickly winning awards at the Royal Bath & West and Devon County Shows, including Supreme Champion at the latter. The vast majority of success has been with ciders that have retained a residual sweetness by arrested fermentation, not through keeving, but through multiple cold rackings. Justin is then able to balance the sweetness through tannins and acidity from a blend of bittersweet, sweet, sharp and bittersharp apples, with long slow fermentations.

Venton's Devon Cyder

Clyst St Lawrence

Standout cider: 2012 Vintage, 6.5%

Style: Bottle-Fermented Cider

Notes: A bit of a rarity this one – 9 years old and triple fermented! Its age, in combination with spending time in oak and being bottle-fermented (twice), provides amazing complexity – blackberry leaf, satsumas and caramel on the smell while bitter orange, lemony Earl Grey tea and raisins dominate the taste.

You can't not like Mark Venton, a builder by trade who brings a fun and optimistic attitude to his cyder making. Based only 2½ miles from the site of the former Whiteway's Cidery, Venton's is all about working with minimal intervention from start to finish. All of the apples they press come from within 6 miles of the cidery, from old, traditional orchards, which facilitates the slow, wild fermentations Mark favours. The cyders, therefore, are characterised by being complex in flavour from the broad blend of varieties that reflects the local landscape and traditions.

Bollhayes Cider

Clayhidon

Standout cider: 2014 Vintage, 8.4% ABV

Style: Bottle-Fermented Cider

Notes: Big, shouty phenolics burst from the glass – allspice, clove, earth, raisins and TCP – while the flavour concentration is dialled up to 11 with Seville orange bitterness and mahogany woodiness.

Bollhayes Cider was founded in 1988 by Alex and his late wife, Bee, and began life as a classic operation providing 5 gallons to enthusiastic traditional drinkers, pubs and festivals. After being inspired by James and Cathy Lane of Gospel Green Cider in Sussex, and using Alex's propensity for scientific accuracy, Bollhayes started production of the bottle-fermented ciders with which they are now synonymous.

Somerset

Without doubt, Somerset is the county that resonates with people most greatly when asked 'Where does cider come from?' Why is this? Firstly, there is the longstanding heritage, like most of the West Country, of making cider on the farm. Interestingly, when cider began to change into the modernised, commercial era, it remained a crux of rural life, unlike those other counties where the farmhouse tradition all but died out. This could be attributed to its proximity to Bristol – a city of great population and a reputation for enjoying the results of the fermented apple. Today it remains the county with the greatest number of traditional makers, some of whom are a bit newer to the game and some with family names that stretch back generations, such as Perry, Wilkins, Rich, Crossman, Hecks, and Sheppy.

Cider (and perry), did, of course, become big business in Somerset, with the likes of Coates, Showerings, Taunton, and latterly, Thatchers, all becoming household names. It was the accompaniment to this expansion in the 1960s of marketing and music that has cemented Somerset's place as the home of cider in the national psyche. The Wurzels' unique brand of folk and country ('Scrumpy and Western'), encouraging folk to 'Drink up thy Zider', and the TV advert proclamation 'Coates comes up from Zummerzet, Where the zoider apples grow' facilitated this.

Although the farmhouse tradition remains strong, there is also now the emergence of makers who wish to build upon the old traditions, and the classic varieties, to bring cider to a whole new contemporary audience.

Barley Wood Orchard

Wrington

Standout cider: Medium Dry, 6.2% ABV

Style: Western Counties

Notes: Amazing and unexpected aromas of honeysuckle and lemongrass hit the nose upon opening, before a wonderful balance of crème caramel sweetness, zippy fresh acidity and grunty bitterness work harmoniously in the mouth.

Mike Atkins and Isy Schulz have always been passionate about people, community, food and fun, so cider seemed a natural fit. Based in the cider house adjacent to the award-winning Ethicurian restaurant on the Barleywood Estate in Wrington, just outside Bristol, these are classic Somerset ciders, expressing the bold tannins of the beloved local varieties. Whether bone dry, keeved, still, sparkling, SV or blended, they make a cider for every taste.

Wilding Cider

Chew Magna

Standout cider: Nempnett Thrubwell, 7% ABV

Style: Western Counties

Notes: Named after the hamlet from which the fruit from this single orchard blend was sourced, this cider is everything you would hope from such an evocative name. The aroma is like walking through a meadow in the height of summer – chamomile florality and oregano herbacousness. Brisk acidity kicks off the taste experience, heightened by the bubbles. This is followed by nutmeg and allspice before a satisfying light astringency sweeps around the mouth.

Sam and Beccy Leach have always been passionate about food and drink, having formerly run the excellent Little Birch restaurant in Bristol. A change of lifestyle beckoned, however, and cider was the answer. They describe themselves as 'orchard cider makers and farmers', using traditional Somerset varieties from their own orchard, as well as from local heritage orchards which they manage in a careful organic way. Fermented gently and slowly with wild yeasts, no sulphites and plenty of time, the ciders are bottled still, or with some kind of natural sparkle.

Honey's Midford Cider

Midford

Standout cider: **Medium Dry Still, 6.2% ABV**

Style: **Western Counties**

Notes: Floral lemongrass and then tamarind on the tongue – sweet, sour and savoury all at the same time. Finishes with a lovely bitterness, but with smooth creamy edges. A must with Thai food.

Established by Bob Honey on his farm in Midford at the turn of the century to revive the orcharding and cider-making culture of the area, Honey's has been synonymous with full-bodied, traditional ciders. The ownership has changed, with Kim Jones now at the helm, but the ethos remains the same – using classic, farm-grown Somerset tannic apples, wild fermenting them, and then packaging them with little added or taken away.

Harry's Cider

Long Sutton

Standout cider: **Dabinett SV, 6% ABV**

Style: **Western Counties**

Notes: This is a cider with a reputation … for greatness! The judges at the Royal Bath & West Show were sufficiently enamoured with it back in 2018 to award it Supreme Champion Cider, and I can understand why. Cleverly back sweetened with unfermented Dabinett juice, this cider oozes orange juice with honeysuckle and caramel softening the edges.

Harry Fry was milking cows for just under 20 years, followed by further years milking 500 goats. However, an ever-fluctuating milk price meant Harry sought a new opportunity to diversify, and so in 2005 he started using formerly contracted apples from the farm to make his eponymously named cider. Harry keeps things simple in the cidery, fermenting and maturing five classic Western Counties apple varieties on their own before blending prior to packaging. The result: a range of award-winning ciders that succeed in achieving that challenging thing – consistent, clean, full-bodied, great tasting cider.

Tricky Cider

Churchstanton

Standout cider: Wizard, 6.5% ABV

Style: Western Counties

Notes: A classic Somerset farmhouse cider. Spicy, medicinal, earthy and baked apple aromas forcibly make their way up the nostrils (in the nicest possible way) before gorgeously smooth, broad, oxidised brioche and raisin characters fill every crevice of your mouth.

Already an established enterprise, rooted in the depths of the Somerset Levels, Matt Gillett took over the business in 2015. He takes a modern, hands-on approach to matters, working with local landowners and farmers, picking a range of varieties and collaborating with other cider makers. This allows them to produce an ever-changing menu providing a wide range of options to everyone from diehard dry lovers to fruit cider enthusiasts.

Sheppy's Cider

Bradford-on-Tone

Standout cider: 2019 Vintage Reserve, 7.4% ABV

Style: Western Counties

Notes: A cider of substance. Afforded longer maturation, and in oak vessels to boot, than the rest of the range. To smell this cider is like stepping into the vat shed itself – dank, brooding and nostril filling. The punchiest of the bittersweet apples at Sheppy's disposal find their home in this blend, including Tremlett's Bitter, which sadly no longer carries sufficient popularity to be made as an SV. Woodiness, sandpapery astringency and a digestions-aiding bitterness are thoroughly enjoyable experiences in the mouth, while being cleverly easy drinking.

Possibly the oldest remaining family cider maker in Britain, David Sheppy is the sixth generation to be making cider since 1816. A success story of Magner's reinvigoration of cider, the enterprise is still undertaken on the family farm, but with shiny new tanks and packaging lines, attesting to the significant growth over the last decade. Using fruit from the farm and other local growers, the ciders are a lesson in making bold, but easy-drinking tannic ciders. They also have a fantastic visitor centre, with a deli, restaurant and public tours all well worth experiencing.

The Newt in Somerset

Castle Cary

Standout cider: Fine Rosé Cyder, 7.6% ABV

Style: Rosé

Notes: Made from the naturally red-fleshed Red Love apple, this is the best rosé cider I have ever tasted. The strawberry, raspberry and floral aromas, and nectarine-drenched, acid-driven taste, are so beguiling that you could easily be mistaken for drinking its vinous inspiration.

From South African magnate, and owner of the acclaimed Babylonstoren winery in Stellenbosch, comes The Newt – one part hotel and one part Somerset theme park. Naturally, if showcasing the finest the county has to offer, cider – or rather cyder – plays its part. Cellar Master Greg Carnell and Head Cyder Maker Paul Ross (formerly Downside cider and perry) team up to make exquisite fine cyders, using temperature control and extreme attention, allied to elegant branding, to create ciders that ooze the characters and value perception of wine.

Crafty Nectar

Shepton Mallet

Standout cider: No.9 Blackberry & Hibiscus Co-Ferment, 4% ABV

Style: Co-Fermentation

Notes: The perfect cider to present to someone who defiantly believes that the addition of other fruits cannot result in a cider of integrity and character. Co-fermenting the blackberries brings out oxidised raisin character which, combined with a restrained quantity of sugar and a bold, grippy tannin base underneath, leads to a balanced, bold and refreshing experience.

The UK's finest cider subscription box service, Crafty Nectar is the brainchild of Ed Calvert and James Waddington. Active and positive participants in the cider community over the last five years, they are on a clear drive to get cider perceived in the same way that craft beer is – fun, creative, contemporary. They also provide a platform for smaller makers to sell their wares online, as well as working with makers to create their own portfolio of ciders, spanning Western Counties, Flavoured, Co-Fermention and Low Alcohol.

Gloucestershire

A county of considerable cider and, especially, perry repute. Much like Devon, this once proud orcharding and farmhouse cider-making county has lost much of its former prowess. The transition from farmhouse to commercial cider making during the early 20th century precipitated a number of small commercial enterprises, none of which still exist, either succumbing to the changes in business practices or being purchased by nearby Bulmers.

Gloucestershire's location led to it not reaching the number of volume scale of makers in Herefordshire, Somerset and Norfolk. Firstly, it had no great route to market. Despite being close to Bristol, the Somerset makers primarily controlled the sale of cider in the city. Secondly, being next to Herefordshire meant that any maker that grew to any competitive scale were soon snapped up by Bulmers and fairly promptly closed down.

Gloucestershire is arguably more closely associated with perry, containing within its boundaries the iconic May Hill – traditionally held as being at the epicentre of 'perry country' – and the place of origin of many of the classic varieties such as Blakeney Red, Oldfield and Taynton Squash. To drive (or even better cycle) down the lanes of Gloucestershire and to see cathedral arched perry pear trees standing proudly in sight of May Hill is a truly magical experience.

Bushel + Peck Cider & Perry

Winchcombe

Standout cider: Cambridge Quoining & Friends, 7% ABV

Style: Eastern Counties

Notes: Not a classic Gloucestershire cider in as much as it isn't tannin forward, but this is a great drink. Big, oily, herbaceous esters rip off the surface and jump right to the top the nose, creating a forward base for the imminent arrival of tastes of menthol, kiwi fruit, creamy lemon curd (MLF at its best) and slate.

One of my favourite new(ish) cider makers of the last few years. After 20 years of corporate life, David Lindgren wanted a change from the office towards something more enjoyable and contributing to sustainable principles; this led him to cider's door. All of the fruit comes from unsprayed trees, including, in 2020, some 5.5 tonnes of unwanted surplus fruit from people's gardens. This use of tannin dominant and acid dominant apples, as well as classic Gloucestershire perry pears, ensures David has a large palette of aromas and tastes to work with.

Severn Cider & Perry

Awre

Standout cider: Medium Sparkling Perry, 5.4% ABV

Style: Classic Perry

Notes: Intense, confected, yummy balsamic aromas lead onto Margarita-like acidity, segueing into ripe pears and passion fruit, all swept up at the end by dusty tannins.

Philip Bull began making cider at the Old Vicarage in Awre (pronounced 'Arrrrr') on the banks of the River Severn in 1956. Today, generations two and three, Nick and Tom respectively, create traditional, wild fermented ciders from classic Western Counties tannic apple varieties. There is a lovely focus on landscape, cultural heritage and orchards. The ciders are bold, robust, chewy and satisfying – sensational with intense, umami-rich food – but it is traditional perry that is their true signature, replete with beautiful woodcut designs evoking the local landscape, May Hill and all.

Dunkertons Cider

Cheltenham

Standout cider: Breakwell's Seedling SV, 7.5% ABV

Style: Western Counties

Notes: This Breakwell's Seedling, an uncommon SV cider, is beautifully heavy weight but gossamer smooth at the same time. The rich, leather, fresh hay and boozy warmth keep it driving very happily all the way to the back of the mouth.

Formally of Herefordshire, but now firmly camped in Gloucestershire, Julian Dunkerton has wonderfully succeeded in his endeavour to ensure that the legacy of his father, Ivor, and step-mother, Susie, as organic cider pioneers continues. Remarkably, the cider-making team have managed to retain the characteristic Dunkertons 'deep flavour' in transition across the county border, leading to a range of phenolic, fruity, weighty ciders.

Wild Cider Co

Wooton-under-Edge

Standout cider: Tyndale Gold, 6.6% ABV

Style: Western Counties

Notes: Freshly cut hay, stone fruits and gentle spice and leather are the hallmark of this cider made from a blend of apples picked under the watchful gaze of Tyndale Monument.

Arguably the finest cider maker in the Cotswolds, John Barnes (no, not the former Liverpool and England footballer) does exactly what it says on the tin – he makes wild fermented, full juice and supremely clean and expressive cider from local fruit.

Making less than 70hl means that Wild Cider isn't often found far from its South Cotswolds epicentre, but it does enable to John to exert full control over the cider and perry he creates, with some truly wonderful results. Brimming with intensity and fruitiness, if ever see a bottle of Wild Cider, grab one!

Jolter Press

Mitcheldean

Standout cider: Squeal, 6% ABV

Style: Western Counties

Notes: The colour is fabulously tawny. Old Jolter could have run his tractor off this. Smell of saddle leather, tar and plum crumble. On the palette there is a remarkable soft, silky, honeycomb juiciness that is just dying to be drunk with tarte tatin.

With a desire to not call his cider enterprise a name containing the words 'orchard' or 'gold', Pat Lock instead wanted to celebrate the culture of the Forest of Dean, and landed upon the story of old Jolter – a man who (allegedly) died of a broken heart in Gloucester Gaol because he missed his native forest so much. The combination of fun, storytelling and the forest runs right through into the cider, too, using a blend of locally sourced fruit to make full juice, wild ferment cider. Jolter would have approved.

Pearson's Cider Co

Moreton-in-Marsh

Standout cider: Dry Cider, 6.7% ABV

Style: Western Counties

Notes: A cider that grows in the mouth and gets better the more you drink. Broad of spicy phenolics on the nose and chewy of tannin in the mouth, eat this with a Rogan Josh and all will be just fine.

Mike Pearson has made cider since 1997 but only commercially since 2013, when the hobby drove a passion so strongly that he decided to quit his job of 25 years in the City and go full time. The bold, clear, contemporary design immediately helped his wares stand out against his competitors, but the liquid also backs it up, straddling those challenging beasts of complexity and accessibility. Although personally enjoying wild fermented cider, Mike uses cultured yeasts to ferment the juice from his blends of tannin-rich apple varieties and keeps everything spotlessly clean.

West Midlands

Although strongly associated with urban sprawl and the Industrial Revolution, the broader West Midlands area includes some the most beautiful landscapes to be found anywhere in Britain. And guess what – cider has been made here for quite a while, and still is today. Quite possibly *the* oldest account of cider making in England comes from Staffordshire, in a record dating back to 1200 which describes a press house and outbuilding with a cider mill, while in 1276 there was a purchase of cider for 20s in Wootton Wawen in Warwickshire.

Worcestershire alone boasts an incredible heritage of orcharding and cider making. The Teme Valley, Vale of Evesham and Wyre Forest are still known today as centres for the growing of cherries, apples, plums and pears. It is this latter fruit that is possibly most closely associated with the West Midlands. Worcestershire is also closely associated with pears and perry, with the town of Pershore – 'Pear-shore' – at its heart. The pear of greatest repute, of course, is the Worcester Black Pear, which can be found on the Worcester City coat of arms, the County Council crest and the cricket and rugby club emblem.

Like so many of the orcharding regions of southern Britain, the West Midlands once had many farmhouse cider (and perry) makers, which have experienced significant decline since the end of the Second World War. Thankfully, though, the heritage and passion for these drinks is kept alive by a band of makers, small and large.

Fletchers Cider

Kidderminster, Worcestershire

Standout cider: Premium Medium Sweet, 6% ABV

Style: Western Counties

Notes: An elegant, gentle and subtle cider. Red apple, raisin and rosehip aromas kicks thing off before gliding through a mid palate of coconut milk and cinnamon, before ending with the gentlest glow of tingly tannins.

Maybe a proud Bristolian such as David France was always going to end up making cider, but doing that in Kidderminster rather than Keynsham changes the narrative slightly. Beginning only in 2016, Fletchers has already accrued a number of awards for their tannic driven ciders which are characterised by their intensity but softness – the result of lengthy maturation and frequent barrel use. In David's own words, 'We call all of our ciders premium as that's what they are!'

Halfpenny Green Cider Company

Stourbridge, Staffordshire

Standout cider: Cidre Charmat, 8% ABV

Style: Western Counties

Notes: Made using the same process as Prosecco, this cider displays a wonderful, toasty, honeycomb and cinnamon aroma and flavour, is creamy smooth with a gently astringent finish and carries the higher alcohol with aplomb. Watch out Prosecco!

Tony Lovering started making cider after a conversation with his barber. Being a process engineer, he was interested in the various processes that could be used to make different naturally sparkling ciders and set out to develop a range that could act as an alternative to sparkling wine. He uses both wild and selected yeasts and has access to a range of varieties that he playfully blends in differing proportions depending on the style he is creating: bottle-fermented, keeved, bottle-conditioned, Pét Nat or Charmat. Tony's ciders all come with a highly extensive checklist on the label as to what has or has not been undertaken or added to the cider – transparency of the highest order.

Hogan's Cider

Alcester, Warwickshire

Standout cider: Libertine, 6.2% ABV

Style: Western Counties

Notes: Surely the most highly awarded cider in the world? In 2019 alone it won gold medals at the International Cider Challenge, International Cider Awards, Cider World and Great Lakes International Cider & Perry Competition. A sticky toffee pudding in a glass – brooding, bittersweet, warming and with caramel sweetness.

No maker succeeds in colouring in the middle bit of the Venn diagram of volume scale and liquid integrity better than Hogan's. Ostensibly a considerably outgrown passion project, Allen Hogan and wife, Jane, in combination with outstanding cider maker Shaun Canavan, create a suite of complex yet accessible cider catering to every palate. They are not shy of being playful either, whether it be with low-alcohol ciders, additional flavours or the use of *Brettanomyces*. Hogan's really are one of cider's great advocates and champions of the last 15 years.

Napton Cidery

Napton-on-the-Hill, Warwickshire

Standout cider: Kingston Black Whiskey Cask, 7.7% ABV

Style: Western Counties

Notes: One of my favourite lockdown ciders, this is a classic Somerset variety matured in an Auchentoshan whisky barrel and made in the West Midlands, and bloody tasty it is, too. There are Christmas pudding levels of clove and cinnamon richness, but finely balanced with a brusque bitterness, dusty astringency and glowing warmth.

A cidery on a steep upward trajectory, Jolyon and Charlotte Oliver are on a mission to bring great cider to the people of the Midlands and far beyond. With a successful crowdfunding behind them, their shiny cidery in the beautiful village of Napton-on-the-Hill is well worth a visit. Here you can observe where the wide range of ciders are made, appealing to all palate preferences, and all using wild yeasts and fruit from traditional orchards.

Robinson's Cider

Tenbury Wells, Shropshire

Standout cider: Premium Medium, 4.8% ABV

Style: Western Counties

Notes: Fresh, fruit salad nose. On the palate is zingy up front – real sherbert dib dabs – which helps to cut through a meringue-like mid palate sweetness.

Technically based a stone's throw over the border in Herefordshire, but included here as the company bears the name of Tenbury Wells (dubbed 'The Town in the Orchard' by Queen Victoria). Angus Robinson is cider-making generation number six from a family of cider makers and pub owners who have been making cider in Tenbury for at least 200 years. He has recently joined the business alongside his father, Robert, and is learning the ropes. At his heart is a desire to tell the unique story of the family, the local cider heritage and of the unsprayed fruit they have at their disposal through the creation of ciders that span the traditional and the contemporary.

Herefordshire

I would say that Herefordshire is the most paradoxical of cider counties. From the 17th century onwards, Herefordshire features in cider literature as the county with the greatest number of orchards and frequently (according to the authors) making the finest quality cider in Britain. Today, it is home to the world's largest cider maker, the world's largest fresh juice fermenting cider maker, as well as a wealth of smaller, traditional, reactionary and progressive producers. And yet, most people have no idea of this. Indeed, many don't even know where the county is, frequently confusing it with the agonisingly similarly-titled Hertfordshire, in the Home Counties.

Why is this the case? Well, geographically speaking, Herefordshire is out the way, en route solely to rural North Wales, home to only one motorway (the M50 – practically a B Road), and being one of the least densely populated regions in England. Crucially, the main Herefordshire maker, Bulmers, did not promote the 'Herefordshireness' of their brands in the same way their Somerset and Devon contemporaries did for their respective counties.

Ironically, it is Herefordshire's location that is such a contributor to its cider success. Being in the lee of the Brecon Beacons and Black Mountains means that it receives considerably less rainfall than Somerset or Devon, while also receiving good sunshine hours and being predominantly overlain by a swathe of rich, fertile, acid clay soils. This terroir is also most conducive to perry, with the majority of makers of this endangered drink operating in the county today.

Ty Gwyn Cider

Pontrilas

Standout cider: Kingston Black SV, 5.8%

Style: Western Counties

Notes: The aroma of this cider is identical to its colour – butterscotch.
A classic indicator of MLF, the creamy theme continues into the palate but is
ably supported by an elegant carbonation, star anise and a slightly medicinal
twang that is so characteristic of ciders made from Kingston Black.

Back in the 1990s Alex Culpin was in a band called Tiny Monroe
that played Glastonbury and supported Radiohead. In Alex's
own words, making music takes 'passion, practice and patience',
skills that ably lend themselves to cider making, which Alex now
undertakes on the Herefordshire side of the Welsh border. Using
locally grown Western Counties apple varieties, Alex favours
making single varieties in a style that makes them easy to drink,
with no rough edges.

Henney's Cider

Bishop's Frome

Standout cider: Dry Cider, 6% ABV

Style: Western Counties

Notes: A fabulous balance between prickly, acidity-raising carbonation,
super creamy diacetyl and neatly puckering astringency.

Mike Henney has worked with cider for a long time, swapping
his Bulmers Marketing Manager role for cider entrepreneur after
some successful test batches back in 1996. At a time when the juice
content of many ciders on the supermarket shelves was lower than
the legal limit today, it was a shining light. And it's still great that
this cider sits on the supermarket shelves, regally holding court
amidst the lurid, coloured jesters sat around it.

Once Upon a Tree Cider & Perry

Ledbury

Standout cider: Bacchus Wine Lees Co-Fermented Cider, 7% ABV

Style: Co-Fermentation

Notes: Want the British version of a Marlborough Sauvignon Blanc? Then look no further. Gooseberry, elderflower and freshly cut hay is followed by a crisp, green apple zing, dried arpricots and satisfying root vegetable sweetness.

A fellow Dymockonian, Simon Day moved back to The Shire back in 2007 after years working as a Jersey winemaker. A daily walk through the neighbouring orchard with the dog led to an enquiry with the proprietors as to whether they would be keen to help him achieve his dream – to make ciders, employing winemaking techniques, that were excellent matches to good food, packaged like wine and that you'd be proud to take to a dinner party and share among friends. The answer was yes, and the business has grown from strength to strength, creating still and carbonated ciders, as well as innovative co-fermentations.

Gregg's Pit Cider & Perry

Much Marcle

Standout cider: Thorn SV 2017 In-bottle-fermented, 7.5% ABV

Style: Bottle-Fermented Perry

Notes: My favourite perry pear variety, which produces huge quantities of aromas and flavours of grapefruit, pineapple and passion fruit. James Mardsen refers to this as a 'breakfast perry', but with the fruit backed up by fabulous pithy bitterness and a soft umaminess, I would say you can enjoy this drink morning, noon or night.

Cider, but especially perry, has been made at Gregg's Pit (the name of the small holding) in Much Marcle for centuries. We can be certain of this because there is a perry pear variety named Gregg's Pit, and the original 'mother tree' is still standing proud, and tall as an oak. James Marsden has been making multi-award-winning cider and perry here since the mid-1990s, initially under the tutelage of Jean Nowell. His drinks, available on draught, but mostly synonymous with being bottled with some kind of natural sparkle, are a byword for excellence, demonstrating the properties of the fruit and of the terroir from which they came.

Newton Court Cider

Newton nr Leominster

Standout cider: Black Mountain Perry, 4.2% ABV

Style: Classic Perry

Notes: Made from a blend of pears but with Newton Court's favourite, Winnal's Longden, at its core, this perry is all about the florality – elderflowers and jasmine – before leading onto a juicy, unctuous, yet beautifully poised drink thanks to light acidity and brisk bubbles.

Paul Stephens's first forays into cider making with his father, Tom, 20 years ago on the family farm in North Herefordshire quickly yielded awards and a reputation for really expressive, fruit-forward ciders and perries. Maybe this shouldn't come as a surprise given the 30 acres of traditional, certified organic apple and pear orchards he has to work with. If you're ever in North Herefordshire, it's well worth stopping by the farm.

Artistraw Cider

Clifford

Standout cider: A la Volée, 6.7% ABV

Style: Western Counties

Notes: Made using the ancestral method (i.e., Pét Nat), but then aged on the lees for 10 months, riddled and then disgorged by hand *à la volée* ('on the fly' in French). This creates a cider with oaky, leathery, gently spicy phenolics and gently chewy tannins.

Living in London, but with Lydia Crimp originating from Somerset and partner Tom Tibbits a keen homebrewer, the lure of cider was enough to relocate these two passionate environmentalists and permaculture advocates out into the wilds of West Herefordshire, a stone's throw from the Welsh border. Here, using fruit from traditional local orchards (while their hand-planted orchard comes to fruition) and applying a minimal intervention approach, they create a range of clean, expressive, predominantly naturally sparkling ciders.

South Coast

This region spans the stylistic West/East divide. Dorset claims far more association with neighbouring Devon and Somerset, from a heritage and cider profile point of view, creating predominantly tannic ciders, though sometimes it's nearer the south coast with a softening, ameliorating effect from the temperate coastline. This rural county can also lay claim to a heritage as old as its more illustrious neighbours, with merchants already active in the 17th century.

The further east one pops along the coast, the cider generally becomes decidedly more fresh and crisp, owing to the predominance of dessert apples used. Hampshire is rapidly gaining a reputation for producing bottle-fermented ciders. The cider heritage in neighbouring West Sussex can be traced back to 1341 when as many as 74 of the 80 parishes were paying their tithes in cider. Although not as prominent today, West Sussex is home to some of the more pioneering cider makers, taking their cue from conventional and natural wine. The Isle of Wight and Guernsey also make an appearance here, showcasing what can be achieved when surrounded by water.

Silly Moo Cider

Horsham, West Sussex

Standout cider: Silly Moo Unfiltered, 5% ABV

Style: Western Counties x Eastern Counties

Notes: Gosh, this is a win! The bold, fun branding slapped on a 330ml can just makes you want to pick it up, crack it open and pour away. Once you taste it, you're not disappointed either. Soft, measured and mid weight, it is perfectly balanced. Gentle, tingly acidity that wants to turn a touch sour, goes skipping along with mangoes and honey-inflected sweetness before a swoosh of soft astringency cleanses the palate ready for the next sip.

This West Sussex cider maker started after Rachel Knowles's parents discovered excellent cider while on holiday in Herefordshire and decided to switch their diversifications plans from grapes to apples on the family beef farm. Taking a minimal intervention approach, in the orchard and the cidery, Rachel's focus is on creating ciders with tannic apples but then backsweeten with with local culinary and dessert apples creating moreish, sessionable ciders.

Rocquette Cider

Guernsey

Standout cider: Traditional, 6% ABV

Style: Western Counties

Notes: A showcase of leathery, medicinal phenolics on the nose ensure we know we're going to expect some tannins on the taste, and they don't disappoint. Interestingly, this is expressed more through bitterness than astringency, adding to the punchiness.

With records of cider being made on the island, and exported to England for centuries no less, it should come as no surprise that great cider is being made on Guernsey. James Meller's family purchased some land on the island in 1998 and wanted to do something innovative and fun, and cider was the answer! They make their cider from their own tannic apples, grown using an unconventional spray-free approach, and combine them with 30 tonnes a year of publicly 'swapped' apples.

Grazed Knee Cider

Ventnor, Isle of Wight

Standout cider: Island Time, 6.5% ABV

Style: Eastern Counties

Notes: I know what you're thinking – does it taste like a cave? The answer ... a little bit! It certainly does have a remarkable minerality and texture to balance with fresh, citrus fruit burst, all enhanced by the bottle conditioning.

Once upon a bike ride, a gravelly puddle became the cause of a fall. Recovering from the grazed knee over a glass of local cider, Helen Jones and Katherine Bouton wondered whether they could produce something so delicious and refreshing. They found themselves an orchard plot, assembled their cidery in a cave under St Boniface Down and thus Grazed Knee Cider was born. The orchard is planted with a collection of local island apple varieties including Isle of Wight Pippin, Sir John Thorneycroft and Bembridge Beauty, as well as classic bittersweet and bittersharp cider varieties and a few varieties with names they couldn't resist such as American Mother and Slack ma Girdle. They blend together juice from the apples to provide the best mix of acidity and tannins before fermenting and maturing in the cool confines of the cave.

Meon Valley Cider

West Meon, Hampshire

Standout cider: Egremont Russet SV, 8.3% ABV

Style: Eastern Counties

Notes: Matured in Sauterne barrels and perfectly bottled conditioned, this cider is simply gorgeous. Smells of jasmine, gun flint and lime sorbet, and tastes of dried apricots, thyme and happiness.

Charlotte and Nigel Johnson's modus operandi at Meon Valley is to make what they seek in the wines they enjoy: tastiness, accessibility and complexity. To achieve this they source local, acid-driven apples, such as Egremont Russet, Cox and Bramley from Hampshire and Sussex, together with Western Counties-sourced Dabinett, Michelin and Yarlington Mill. As they continue their cider journey they are continually trying new things, such as maturing on oak chips, bottle conditioning and, in conjunction with Portsmouth Distillery, are about to launch an eau de vie.

Gospel Green Cyder

Blackmoor, Hampshire

Standout cider: Gospel Green Original Cyder, 8.4% ABV

Style: Bottle-Fermented Cider

Notes: Bottle fermented with enough time *sur lie* to develop delicate brioche characters, but not too long to obscure the inherent florality and green apple aromas. Crisp, with a light acidity and a slight earthiness coming through on the palate. Smooth with a rounded finish and a long-lasting mousse.

The name Gospel Green is synonymous with fine, bottle-fermented cyder. The company was established in 1990 by James and Cathy Lane who wanted to showcase that the apple had as much to offer as the grape when it came to sparkling drinks. Brock Bergius, a customer of Gospel Green, was so distraught when being told the business was looking to be wound down in 2016 that he promptly bought it himself! Brock continues James and Cathy's legacy of excellence, now operating from the Blackmoor Estate in Hampshire and allowing direct access to some of the finest apples in the country.

Chalkdown Cider

Andover, Hampshire

Standout cider: Extra Lees Aged 2014, 8.2% ABV

Style: Bottle-Fermented Cider

Notes: This is all about the bubbles, which accentuate the sensations of crunchy apples, brioche, toast, pastry and vanilla, with a hint of apple pie.

The ethos and approach to cider making at Chalkdown is entirely informed by Champagne, maybe not surprising given that cider maker Piotr Nahajski is also a trained wine maker and fan of robust, bottled-fermented wines. Right on his doorstep he has the varieties that suit his needs of higher acidity and lower tannin perfectly. The crisp fruitiness of Cox's Orange Pippin and the sugar and nuttiness of Egremont Russet are the mainstays, but also, depending on the vintage, Braeburn, Bramley, Spartan and Kanzi, among others. The ciders are then lain down for a minimum of 18 months before disgorging.

Rebel Root Cider Works

Bolney, West Sussex

Standout cider: Down Time, 4.5% ABV

Style: Eastern Counties

Notes: The branding has all of the colour and vibrancy of a craft beer, but is all cider on the inside. A cacophony of fresh herbs on the nose, in the mouth we have citrus, yeasty texture and cheese rind earthiness. If you're into UK sour-style Saison beers then give this a go.

Another great example of the next generation breathing life into an orchard-based family farm, trying to navigate its way in an increasingly tough commercial landscape, Tom Stephens is making a difference to West Sussex-based Wobblegate Orchards through his Rebel Root cider brand, and through the on-site Cider Tap. Experimentation, innovation and challenging perceptions is the order of the day for Tom, with all of his 750ml bottled range being still, dry, and wild yeast fermented interpretations of the humble Bramley. Rebel Root also has two recent canned releases, in 440ml, dry and sparkling. More casual and crushable, but still complex in their story, creation and purpose.

Cranborne Chase Cider

Blandford Forum, Dorset

Standout cider: Smuggler, 6% ABV

Style: Western Counties

Notes: The perfect cider to give to someone as they undergo their dry cider journey – low on sugar, big on bitterness, creamy smoothness and apple pie-soft fruitiness.

Such did Bill Meaden miss cider on his global travels that when he returned to his old stomping ground of North Dorset he set about making amends through establishing his own business. Named after the Area of Outstanding Natural Beauty within which it sits, Cranborne Chase Cider is focused on upholding the local cider-making traditions, while also making ciders that appeal to a contemporary crowd. They also describe themselves as low input, sustainable cider makers, running their cider shed and press from solar power, and with a focus on managing their orchards in a responsible way for the health of the trees and the wildlife around them.

The South-East

It should come as no surprise that the region containing the Garden of England should come with some considerable cider repute. Indeed, Giraldus Cambrensis tells us that the monks of Canterbury preferred cyder to Kentish ale back as far as the 12th century.

Owing to the favourable dry climate and proximity to London, the growing of apples was taken to a whole new level with Richard Harris, fruiterer to King Henry VIII, investing in a substantial nursery in Teynham in 1533. Today, the South-East remains crucial in the British top fruit industry, with 44% of all apples and pears in the UK grown in this region, and in Kent also resides Brogdale – home of the National Fruit Collection.

Cider making in the South-East, using dessert and culinary apples to create fresh, clean acid driven ciders like their Western and Eastern counterparts, would have formed an integral part of the agricultural community, before much of it was lost in the 20th century. A few names, like Luck's and Merrydown, persevered for a while, but the legacy is being upheld today by a new wave of makers, once again realising the full potential of the quality fruit they have on offer. Some take a lead from craft brewers, creating ciders of vibrant aesthetics and contemporary packaging, whilst others take their cues from the multitude of neighbouring award-winning wine makers. The result is a joyousness and technical quality of cider making that is as good as they come in Britain.

Kentish Pip

Canterbury, Kent

Standout cider: High Diver, 4.8% ABV

Style: Eastern Counties

Notes: The epitome of Kentish cider. Mineral Cox and sharp Bramley marry and meld with the sweetness to provide a crisp, fresh, smooth, easily drinkable can of loveliness.

Everything revolves around the family fruit farm in Woolton, just outside Canterbury, for Kentish Pip's Sam Mount. His dad got him interested in making cider around 2012 and he was sufficiently fascinated by the process that he left his job and went full time into cider in 2016. Their clear desire is to make drinks for people to enjoy while not being too evangelical about tradition. To achieve their great range of styles they use a combination of tannic, culinary, heritage and modern dessert apples.

Luke's Cider

London

Standout cider: Original Sin 2019, 5.5% ABV

Style: Western Counties

Notes: This cider oozes hay barn-fresh florality, but tastes like the most joyous and juicy of fruit salads, all guava and Alfonso mango. The mouthfeel is soft, the sweetness is gentle and the vibes are good. This cider has immense crushability.

Having finished university, not feeling much inspiration to pursue a career in the subjects he studied, and with an eye on the burgeoning craft beer scene, London-based Luke McCoy decided to investigate whether cider could be next in line for the same treatment. After gaining experience in Herefordshire, Somerset and Normandy, he took the plunge in 2015 and made his first batch of cider, sourcing fruit from western England and making it in the Big Smoke. Using a minimal intervention approach to his cider making, Luke's primary point of difference is that he was (to my knowledge) the first craft/small cider maker to place his drink into a 330ml can, taking a lead from craft beer, and using the format to act as a canvas for fun, modern artwork.

Turners Cider

Marden, Kent

Standout cider: Russet SV, 8% ABV

Style: Eastern Counties

Notes: This cider has the reassuringly expected 'nutty' aromas of classic russeted apples, but with unexpected passion fruit and clematis flower joining the party. The Christmas nut selection runs through this from front to back, from a touch of walnut bitterness to cherry almond smoothness to a boozy Frangelico finish. Outstanding.

Inspired by Somerset friends running a community orchard and making cider, and a desire to escape London for the good life, led May and Phil Turner to decamp to mid Kent, where they borrowed a press, read some books and juiced their first apples. The entrepreneurial spirit was fired up and Turners Cider was born. Today it makes 100% juice fermented ciders, using locally grown dessert and culinary apples and pears from south-facing organic orchards. The fruit is picked by hand, then pressed and fermented in stainless steel vats to create clean, fruity and expressive ciders.

Ascension Cider Co

Polegate nr Eastbourne, East Sussex

Standout cider: Voss Kveik Fermented SV Russet, 8.3% ABV

Style: Eastern Counties

Notes: The exception to the wild ferment rule is a most exceptional cider indeed. The natural nutty and textural propensities of an SV Russet are taken in a whole new direction by the use of a Norwegian beer yeast – Voss Kveik – which ferments at high temeratures and imparts big umami savouriness, alongside orange peel and melon.

A third- generation hot air balloon pilot with a passion for cider, Matt Billing established Ascension Cider Co back in 2017 and is now based in an old apple store on an orchard in East Sussex. Over 20 varieties of dessert and culinary apples are grown here, meaning they're never short of ingredients and inspiration. They use the 'batch methodology' – taking fruit out of cold store all year round to ferment and mature on short timescale to ensure freshness is retained. The ciders are (nearly) all wild fermented and backsweetened with juice.

Starvecrow Cyder

Rye, East Sussex

Standout cider: Starvecrow Natural Cyder 2019, 5.5% ABV

Style: Eastern Counties

Notes: This is as close to an Asturian *sidra natural* or Basque *sagardoa* as you will find in Britain today. Starts with lightly yeasty, citrusy nose and in the mouth it follows with green celery, grapefruit bitterness and mouth coating, barrel-induced texture. Drink with something fatty to cut through.

The result of a collaboration between acclaimed natural wine maker Ben Walgate (Tillingham Wine) and farmer Steve Reeve, Starvecrow takes its cues very heavily from minimal intervention wine. These are 100% juice ciders, in the truest sense of the term, wild fermented and made from Golden Delicious, Braeburn, Bramley and Jonagold, and are often naturally condition and/or allowed to spend time maturing in wooden vessels imparting a flavour.

The Orchard Project

London

Standout cider: Local Fox Medium, 6.2% ABV

Style: Eastern Counties

Notes: I swear this cider tastes even better knowing that it is made from fruit that was either unwanted or coming from community orchards in and around London. If one could smell a colour, this would beer the most vibrant of greens. The dollop of sweetness not only helps to balance with the searing acidity, but really helps to enhance the nectarine and orange juice characters.

The Orchard Project was established in 2009 as the only national charity dedicated solely to the creation, restoration and celebration of community orchards. They aim to make a serious contribution to a better food system, based on people working together where they live to produce and harvest their own fruit. In a bid to reduce food waste and undertake a commercial enterprise, cider making has been in operation for five years now. In that time they have rescued 38 tonnes of unused fruit, engaged with 17 orchards and trained 1,300 volunteers across 171 events!

Hawkes Cidery and Taproom

London

Standout cider: Pineapple Punch, 4% ABV

Style: Flavoured (Fruit)

Notes: Like a Pina Colada in a can. The party really gets started in the mouth with salty, tingly acidity not being overwhelmed by sweetness. Wonderfully refreshing.

Not even a decade old, the now Brewdog-owned Hawkes has made a considerable contribution to cider's betterment in that time. Making and slinging cider in London's Craft Beer HQ, changing perceptions and taste buds along the way, they also provide the capital with its primary opportunity to view cider making, bringing the story of cider to the drinkers. They are an integral part of the modern British cider story.

The South

The broader Home Counties area certainly is recorded as being widely planted in medieval times with orchards used to make cider and perry. Of particular note is the Warden pear, thought to have been selected by the Cistercian Monks of Warden Abbey. Such is its hardness, and challenging taste, it was known to have been turned into perry. However, many of the old orchards were not replanted by the 17th century, the reason being, as in Kent and Sussex, the profitability of growing table fruit for the ever-expanding London market.

Any traditional cider making all but died with this trend, which can also be said of Oxfordshire. The county can lay claim, however, to being home to one of cider's great 17th-century advocates, Ralph Austin. He was a prominent horticulturalist, growing and selling apple trees from the centre of Oxford, and set out his vision of the joy of cider in his 1653 book, *A Treatise on Fruit Trees*.

Wiltshire is an entirely different proposition. With its western edge bordering onto Gloucestershire, Somerset and Dorset, it surely must have had at one time a tradition not unlike its more illustrious neighbours. Alas, this has not transitioned into the modern era, and there is a paucity of makers today.

Pang Valley Cider

Cold Ash, Berkshire

Standout cider: Royal County II, 5.3% ABV

Style: Eastern Counties

Notes: Playful, elegant and just plain old yum! A blend of wild and wine yeast ferments, the Jonagold and Spartan components provide fabulous parma violet and bubblegum perfumed aromas, while the Cox and Russet give structure, and tastes of rhubarb and custard.

One of my greatest discoveries during the challenging lockdown period was Pang Valley Cider, a name I hadn't yet come across. The company was only established in 2018 by Rick Wyatt and Gary Wickens and uses local dessert fruit, as well as tannic fruit from further west, to produce classic Eastern Counties and Western Counties styles, as well as keeved ciders. Regardless of style, the hallmark across all their ciders is cleanliness, freshness and intensity, like the flavour has been dialled up to 11. I'd urge you to seek them out.

Green Shed Cider

Newbury, Berkshire

Standout cider: Two Wheels, 5% ABV

Style: Eastern Counties x Western Counties

Notes: A cider with amazingly broad, smooth tannins coming from Vilberie, a late bittersweet apple sourced from Herefordshire. This has been balanced with Prince William and a blend of other acid-driven apples to provide fruitiness, although much of the original brisk acidity has dropped away to creaminess thanks to MLF.

The brainchild of David Bailey, the ethos at Green Shed is simplicity – using 100% juice and minimising the addition of anything else to create accessible and interesting ciders. Part two of the cider-making ethos is fun, with David regularly getting friends and the local community to help pick and press. Rather wonderfully, as a testament to the rigours of making cider by hand, David describes his ciders as being 'graft' rather than 'craft'. I quite like it!

Shed Cider

Bromham, Wiltshire

Standout cider: Dry Still, 6% ABV

Style: Western Counties

Notes: Smoother than a Teflon-coated ferret, this cider glides through palate, slowly increasing in weight and texture, dropping grenades of orange peel and liquorice along the way. The blend of very low acid and super ripe bittersweet apples, combined with MLF, gives the impression of sweetness, even when there isn't any.

Amazingly, and sadly, the only Wiltshire cider maker to feature in this book. After a lifetime of good health, in April 2017 Roger Blake was incapacitated due to a slipped disc. He contemplated the meaning of life and found that the answer was converting his cider making hobby into his profession. Roger entered his very first ciders into the Royal Bath & West Show in 2019 and won gold for 'Best Newcomer to the Industry', and silver for the sweet farmhouse cider in an open class. Something tells me this isn't beginner's luck.

Garden Cider Co

Chiddingfold, Surrey

Standout cider: Elderflower, 4% ABV

Style: Flavoured (Fruit)

Notes: Elderflower and light, fresh, fruit-forward ciders complement each other so well, and this cider does not disappoint. As well as the obvious perfume, the palate, although quite sweet, has a nice, crisp, sherbet and wood herbaceousness to balance.

Surrey isn't commonly associated with cider, but there are certainly plenty of apple trees tucked away in people's gardens, their fruit dropping to the ground with the likely culmination of rotting in situ or being taken to the tip. Will and Ben Filby didn't like the sound of this, so in 2010 established the Garden Cider Co, making all their cider from spare, unwanted garden fruit, with the donators, currently topping 4,000, being repaid in the form of cider. A real win-win, and sustainability in action.

Tutt's Clump Cider

Bradfield, West Berkshire

Standout cider: Kingston Black, 5.5% ABV

Style: Western Counties

Notes: Looks, pours and tastes just like an orange wine. It's all spicy, smoky and medicinal – classic KB – but with a wonderfully racing acidity, chewy tannins and a remarkable confected cherry brightness.

Tim Wale was born in the hamlet of Tutt's Clump, West Berkshire, and still lives there to this day. He has been making cider commercially since 2006 and is ably assisted by his wife and five daughters, two of whom are full-time in the cider business. Although he doesn't care for flavoured ciders, being a self-proclaimed traditionalist, he is a pragmatist and creates a portfolio of flavoured ciders to sit alongside those more fresh and sharp (including some SV like Jazz and Fuji) as well as ciders from tannic apples. They do not filter, pasteurise or carbonate any of their cider, only adding sucralose and sulphites in small quantities.

Cotswold Cider Co

Coleshill, Oxfordshire

Standout cider: Blow Horn, 4% ABV

Style: Flavoured (Botanicals)

Notes: One of my favourite flavoured ciders, this is the original British Chai-spiced cider, and the cardamom really punches through. It has a great tannic base underneath which it marries with slight acidity and modest sweetness, achieving a remarkable body for low such a low ABV.

A spot of home cider making and an opportunity to purchase a 4-acre orchard led Rory Souter down the professional cider path in 2009 and thus the Cotswold Cider Co (CCC) was born. Other than the accessible, fresh cider, the primary things that set these ciders apart from their contemporaries are the fun, bold branding and the early adoption of cans as a means of appealing to a younger, craft beer audience. The ethos of the CCC today is for more people to drink better cider. Amen to that.

The East

The eastern parts of England have as equally a strong heritage of apple growing and of making cider as their western counterparts, but are often overlooked. We can go back as far 1204 to see records of 'the wine of pearmains' (a type of apple) being used to pay the rent.

Britain's oldest continued cider (cyder) enterprise, Aspall of Suffolk, was established by Clement Chevallier in 1728. Aspall was also the world's oldest family owned cider maker until their sale to Molson Coors in 2018. Today, Aspall is still a good bet for an easily found supermarket cider.

Although Bulmers are credited as being the key modernisers of British cider, they were not the first. That title goes to Gaymers of Banham, Norfolk. John Gaymer in all probability began making and selling cider in the 1770s or 1780s, amongst myriad others in the area. The crucial step change, however, was purchasing a hydraulic press in 1870 and becoming a full-time cider enterprise, some 17 years before Percy Bulmer established his cider-making company.

What is so unique about this region, and what differentiates it from the Western Counties, is the use of acid, fresh dessert apples rather than tannic apples. This gives the opportunity, if made well, for these ciders to display the aromatic, flavour and textural character of white wine. Indeed, *The Lancet* of 20 April 1901 reported tasting a dry cider that 'might easily pass for a light Sauterne wine'. Today, the cultural heritage of cider making and fruit growing is upheld by the 30-plus small-scale producers in the region.

Skidbrooke Cyder Co

Nr Louth, Lincolnshire

Standout cider: General Ludd Medium, 6% ABV

Style: Eastern Counties

Notes: Another great example of the enjoyment of the packaging not being entirely commensurate with the drinking experience. Fun, finessed and totally unexpected – my favourite kind of cider experience. In the glass you could be forgiven for mistaking this for a White Rioja or Albarano wine.

Cider runs through Guy Williams's veins, with an aunt formerly running a (now sadly closed) cider house in Taunton, and he brings this pedigree to the fore in his cyders made in the boondocks of East Lincolnshire. His ethos is to make the best cider in the world without compromise. For him, this means 100% juice fermented from local dessert and culinary apples with wild yeast and the addition of sucralose (if necessary) for sweetening.

The Big Bear Cider Mill

Sisted, Essex

Standout cider: Essex Gold Rush, 5.4% ABV

Style: Eastern Counties

Notes: Dancing on the borders of being *sidra*-esque, this cider is packed full of juiciness, fruit salad aromas and tingly, refreshing malic acidity. If you're a sour beer fan, give this a go!

Once upon a time, Essex was blessed with orchards, but they were largely ripped up to make way for gravel pits in the 1960s and 1970s. Mark Hughes, aka The Big Bear, always intended to *go large* and is now on a mission to champion the apple once more, having planted up a 500-tree orchard of tannic varieties, and then using this fruit, plus locally sourced dessert apples, to make fresh and easy-drinking ciders. All of their ciders have the prefix Essex Gold – the colloquial name for gravel in the region and a nod to the regenerated gravel pits on which their orchards are planted.

Whin Hill Norfolk Cider

Wells-next-the-Sea, Norfolk

Standout cider: Medium Sparkling, 6.8% ABV

Style: Eastern Counties

Notes: Like walking through an English country garden in June, the aromas are floral and herby. The palate is dominated by a heather honey, milkshake sweetness which is punctuated by some lightly grippy tannins.

Lisa and Mark Jarvis took on the Whin Hill Cider Co back in 2012, and continue the ethos of previous owners, Jim Ferguson and Pete Lynn – cider grown and produced on the Norfolk coast. Having access to classic local dessert and culinary apples, as well as tannic varieties and perry pears, Lisa and Mark are able to achieve a broad range – blends or SVs and across the sweetness spectrum thanks to the addition of juice back to the fermented cider.

Brooks & Conquest Cyder

Huntingdon, Cambridgeshire

Standout cider: Devil's Dyke Medium Sweet, 7.1% ABV

Style: Eastern Counties

Notes: This is, quite literally, a wild cider. It has effectively undergone a degree of acetification, but in an engagingly clean way, which, cleverly combines with the sweetness to enhance the treacle, salty and balsamic characters. This is the Duchesse du Bourgogne of ciders.

Over the course of a (particularly productive) haircut with barber Peter Brooks, Mark Conquest decided that making cyder could be the answer to what to do with the fruit from the family's aged organic orchard that was no longer being taken by the supermarkets. Together they teamed up to form Brooks & Conquest, making East Anglian-style cyder from dessert and culinary apples, all presented in 750ml swing-top bottles and designed to be sipped not glugged. They use the descriptive 'Grand Cru' as this translates from French into 'Great Growth' given much of the fruit is grown on the vigorous M25 rootstock.

East Midlands

From an apple perspective, the East Midlands is most synonymous with the Bramley apple. Grown from a pip planted by young Mary Anne Brailsford somewhere between 1809 and 1815, it flourished to become the most popularly grown and consumed cooking apple in the UK, today accounting for around 94% of all culinary apples grown.

Bramley isn't the only variety associated with the region, of course. There are evocative names such as Marriage Maker (Leicestershire), Winter Quarrenden (Nottinghamshire), Thorpe's Peach (Northamptonshire) and Lamb's Pippin (Derbyshire). Ray Blockley from Torkard Cider in Hucknall, Nottinghamshire, states, 'there were many orchards in the county of Nottinghamshire and the wider region with dedicated sidings and trains to take apples directly to the markets of London[...] So, they weren't true cider apples but no one is going to tell me that someone in the county didn't use them to make cider of some kind or other.'

Today, East Midlands makers use a combination of locally grown dessert, culinary and, increasingly, tannic, apples, as well as buying in some fruit from out west. The fact there are more than 20 makers, plus the planting of new orchards, is testament to the growing interest in cider making in the East Midland. Kudos should be given to Mark Shirley who was a regional pioneer with his Rockingham Forest Cider, encouraging other regional folk to get into making cider and perry in a 'traditional' style but with an eye always on good practice and quality.

Kniveton Cider Co

Kniveton, Derbyshire

Standout cider: Scorchio! 7.5% ABV

Style: Western Counties x Eastern Counties

Notes: Channelling super-clean and clear fruit flavours, on one hand this cider is incredibly delicate and on the other quite robust. A great example of the WestCo x EastCo then! The first hints of pleasing caramelising oxidisation are a welcome addition to the lean, malic acidity, gentle MLF creaminess and softly puckering astringency.

Following a pub conversation with friends back in 2013 about how much fruit from the village's trees went to waste, Kev Wooley spotted an apple press for sale and took it home to his partner, Hannah Barton, and Kniveton Cider Co was born. Their ethos is low intervention and full juice, and they describe themselves as a 'circular business', using primarily dessert and culinary fruit that would have otherwise gone to waste – although they do buy a small quantity of some locally grown tannic apples. This translates into their ciders being still and mostly bone dry.

Torkard Cider Company

Hucknall, Nottinghamshire

Standout cider: Straight Outta Hucknall, 6.5% ABV

Style: Eastern Counties

Notes: This cider has electrifying green apple acidity coming from a decent dash of cooking apples. Smells like wheatgrass and thyme, tastes like tangfastics, quince and dandelions. If you're a fan of bone dry Riesling, give this a crack.

A former CAMRA stalwart, including running the Nottingham Robin Hood Festival Cider Bar, Ray Blockley now continues his cider advocacy in an independent capacity, and alongside wife, Gail, through the Torkard Cider Company. One of the East Midlands' modern-day cider pioneers, Torkard Cider uses 100% freshly pressed apple juice from the home orchard in Hucknall and from other Nottinghamshire orchards. They have literally nothing done or added to them, save for a drop of sucralose if the consumer demands a touch of sweetness, so all of their ciders are presented still and live.

Charnwood Cider

Anstey, Leicestershire

Standout cider: Dabinett SV Full Juice Dry, 8.4% ABV

Style: Western Counties

Notes: Welcome To Dabinett. This cider is a lot of fun, but certainly not for the faint-hearted. Intense hardy herbs – think sage and thyme – marry with Seville orange bitterness, dried apricot fruitiness, a rasping astringency and a chocolate liqueur finish.

Rob Clough rather neatly describes his approach to cider making as not scientific, but physical. And with an orchard of 300 trees to maintain, and making cider with a minimal intervention approach, there's plenty of opportunity for physicality! Interestingly, alongside classic bittersweet varieties, the orchard contains some Danish varieties too (sent over by his brother who was working there at the time of planting), including Ingrid Marie and Goldborg. Although a proponent of SV ciders, he does so not because he necessarily thinks they make better cider, but more as a process and learning tool.

Saxby's Cider

Wellingborough, Northamptonshire

Standout cider: Plum Cider, 4% ABV

Style: Flavoured (Fruit)

Notes: A reassuring, burnt-gold colour (rather than radioactive pink) assures the realness of the fruity situation here. Super-clean, fresh, with aromas of pain au raisin and the juiciest of fleshy stone fruits in the mouth, acidity and sweetness balancing nicely.

What does an arable farmer looking for diversification do to make life a little more interesting? Make cider, of course! And so, with some money left to him by his grandmother, Phil Saxby started making cider. The Saxby philosophy on cider is that it doesn't have to be mass produced and homogenous and neither does it have to be too specialised and inaccessible for everyone to appreciate. 'Cider for All' is his philosophy. Using a blend of dessert and bittersweet apples, Phil majors on fruit flavoured ciders, which he insists is 'not a dirty word' given that he uses real fruit juices for a flavour that is subtle and not too sweet.

Blue Barrel Cider

Nottingham

Standout cider: Smoking Barrels, 6.5% ABV

Style: Eastern Counties

Notes: The smells proffers lemon curd and honeysuckle, which transcends into the best of MLF in the mouth – creamy, buttery, smoothness, with a gentle stone fruit and tongue furriness to finish.

It was a visit to the Ross-on-Wye Cider & Perry Co on their honeymoon back in 2011 that spurred Emma and Leo Jordan to turn a hobby into something more professional. This couple has long worked from the land and have a strong community focus, and thus acquire their apples from small holdings, growing projects, urban areas and forgotten orchards to make their 100% juice cider. They've also made it their mission to rewild urban areas (parks, schools, social housing community projects) with fruit trees, which benefits everone.

Cidentro Cider House

Melton Mowbray, Leicestershire

Standout cider: Rosé, 8% ABV

Style: Rosé

Notes: How many fruits is it possible to taste in a cider? A few in this case! A blend of cider and Pinot Noir wine, this is all about stewed plums and peaches mixed with hints of green apples, brooding blackberries and floral raspberries. Perfect summer's day drink for Elevenses.

More accustomed to pork pies than pippins, Melton Mowbray is nevertheless home to a cider maker producing fun and elegant drinks. Planting up an orchard on an old ridge and furrow meadow behind their house back in 2016 signalled the start of the cider journey for Hiranthi and Matthew Cook, looking for something to connect them back the land. They quickly discovered that making smaller quantities of elegant, refined drinks rather than larger volumes was going to be the path for them, and they have started with a bang, creating ciders that could easily be a substitute for wine on the table.

Loxley Cider

Southwell, Nottinghamshire

Standout cider: Rosehip & Sloe, 3.5% ABV

Style: Flavoured (Fruit)

Notes: This is the antidote to the accusations that all fruit ciders are fake and full of sugar. Packed full of hand-picked rosehips and sloes, it really does smell like a hedgerow in autumn, and harmonises rather wonderfully on the palate. It's quite an impressive feat to create a cider of complexity, softness, fruitiness and yet remain defiantly cidery, and all at under 4%.

After spending many years living in Bath, James Parker had become a true lover of cider. However, frustrated by the lack of aspiration he saw in the market, he challenged himself to create a concept of what he thought a modern cider brand might look and feel like. Loxley Cider is the result. The ethos is to honour the history of cider while at the same time creating his own path. This is undertaken by combining an authentic liquid, using local varieties such as Howgate Wonder and classic bittersweets, with a contemporary design created by artist and illustrator Brian Grimwood.

The North

The heritage of apples and cider isn't restricted to the southern half of England. There is an account of cider being made near Richmond, North Yorkshire, back in 1275. But the Yorkshire heritage of orchards and cider continues to the present day. William Lawson's 1618 book, *New Orchard and Kitchen Garden* gives precise instructions for making cider, while, some forty years later, Sir Paul Neile wrote his remarkable treatise on bottle-fermented cider for the Royal Society, based on his experience in his own orchard at Hutton Bonneville in North Yorkshire.

Of course, Yorkshire doesn't make up the entirety of 'The North'. From Bolton to Berwick-upon-Tweed and everywhere in between, fruit has been, and is still being, grown in orchards and walled gardens, with some of it being converted into cider. Thankfully, more trees are being planted and supported through organisations such as The Northern Fruit Group.

Today there is a healthy number of makers right across the North, though the majority are in Yorkshire. They make a range of styles: Eastern Counties, Western Counties, Classic Perry, New World Perry and bottle-fermented iterations of the above. Across the Pennines, largely through the actions of progressive advocates, and Manchester Cider Club founders Dick Withecombe and Cath Potter, Manchester has become cider's capital in the North, and is arguably home to Britain's most active and important cider scene. Bristol, you have been warned!

Dunham Press Cider

Dunham Massey, Cheshire

Standout cider: Red Eye Medium Sweet, 6.2% ABV

Style: Eastern Counties x Western Counties

Notes: This cider has the most gorgeous, luscious leathery smell – like standing in a leather workshop. But it is defined by the rich, golden syrup-like sweetness and gentle bitter finish. Very smooth and very lovely.

Chris Hewitt has been refining his cider making skills on the Dunham Massey National Trust Estate near Altrincham since 2009. He initially started with local dessert apples, but desired the depth and richness of the cider he enjoyed from the South-West, so set about planting up his own orchard of bittersweets and bittersharps, now totalling 23 acres. His ethos is 'bare root to bottle' – justifiably so given he has planted every tree by hand – culminating in him creating full juice ciders that demonstrate the year-on-year variations experienced in the orchard. One of the true pioneers of contemporary Northern cider making, Chris is an integral part of the Manchester cider scene and has won multiple awards for his libations.

Temperance Street Cider

Manchester

Standout cider: Black Dabinett SV, 6.9% ABV

Style: Western Counties

Notes: This is big! Meaty gunflint (a good thing) on the nose leads onto an acidic circus – lemon peel, grapefruit and apricots, with pink peppercorn spice taking over, before a smooth, mellow finish.

Carrying on the legacy of the now defunct but pioneering Moss Cider Project is Temperance Street Cider – Manchester's first city centre cidery. Accepting donated fruit from local gardens and allotments, as well as using select apples for a series of SV ciders, this is the embodiment of what urban cideries are about – community focused, unencumbered by tradition, and creative. This extends to a series of fruit wines, and lower alcohol fruit ciders, also sourced from the local environs.

Mosser Cider

Mosser, Cumbria

Standout cider: Dab Tom Vintage 2018, 6.5% ABV

Style: Western Counties

Notes: A gently perfumed nose gives no indication of the incredible boldness to come –
big umami savouriness, mouth-puckering astringency and Campari levels of bitterness.

Nestled on the edge of the Lake District National Park, Mosser Cider
is taking the 'western' part of Western Counties to its northern
extremity. Growing apples here is, according to Mosser cider maker
Mark Evens, challenging yet rewarding. The reward, in my opinion,
goes to the drinkers who seek out this range of remarkably bold
and flavoursome ciders, made using a range of varieties including
bittersweets such as Dabinett, as well as local favourites like Ribston
Pippin and European classics like Belle de Boskoop.

Thornborough Cider

Thornborough, North Yorkshire

Standout cider: Thornborough Sparkling Cider, 6.9% ABV
Style: Bottle-Fermented Cider

Notes: Rhubarb-like acidity, plus flavours of freshly cut grass and menthol herbaceousness
make this the ultimate refresher.

Kingsley Ash, in his own words, randomly moved up to the rural idyll
of North Yorkshire from London. Introducing himself as an electronic
music producer didn't facilitate easy conversations with the locals,
but his discovery of cider did start to allow connection to people and
to a sense of place. 'People started saying "we have apples". And then
when you start planting trees it really roots you.' Creating his first
batch for his wedding in 2009, and never having been a beer drinker,
Kingsley clearly saw high-value, cider-as-sparkling wine as his niche
within the cider world, and he's doing pretty well having been the
recent recipient of the Sandford Orchard's Breakthrough Cider
Award in 2021.

'Udders Orchard Cider

Huddersfield, West Yorkshire

Standout cider: Luddite, 6.3% ABV

Style: Eastern Counties x Western Counties

Notes: Made with a blend of dessert, culinary and Dabinett bittersweet apples, this cider has a little bit of everything: brisk gooseberry acidity, hazel nuttiness and softly bitter, savoury finish.

Demonstrative of cider's slow filtering into the public concsciousness as a drink of intrigue, 'Udders Orchard has grown mightily in scale from the first pressing in 2008 to where it sits today with its own premises, shop and taproom. Cider maker Dave Kendall-Smith uses local dessert and culinary apples, largely from the gardens and unused orchards of Huddersfield and surrounds, plus a few South-West sourced bittersweets to create a range of wild fermented, full juice ciders brimming with intensity.

Colemans Cider Co

Driffield, East Riding of Yorkshire

Standout cider: Medium Batch #1, 6% ABV

Style: Eastern Counties

Notes: An easy-drinking Eastern Counties-style cider that uses a blend of culinary, dessert and crab apples to create a smooth, still, rich, plum pudding of a cider.

Colemans started when a couple of boys from the West Country came up to Yorkshire and found an abundance of apples but not many Yorkshire ciders available, so they decided to do something about it. The homebrew hobby grew into a small cottage industry and is now producing 30,000 litres each year. All produce for their Yorkshire cider and fruit cider is sourced within the region and is fruit that otherwise would have gone to waste. The single variety range is made from juice sourced from a small family orchard in Herefordshire, enabling them to showcase a diversity of styles and flavours.

Wales

Mother Nature has no truck with geopolitical boundaries and so the landscape of Monmouthshire, Brecon, Radnor and Powys is equally as replete with gnarled orchards, ancient varieties of apple and pear, and old twin screw presses as on the English side of the wiggly line. The heritage here is old, and unique, too. A two-year research project, completed in 2019, identified 73 'new' Welsh specific varieties, boasting wonderful names such as Tanat Reviver and Jac y Do (the Welsh word for Jackdaw).

So strong is this identity that there is even a Protected Indication for the term 'Traditional Welsh Cider/Perry'. This designation ensures that products proudly bearing this label must adhere to certain conditions, which consists of only being allowed to be made from 100% fresh pressed juice and nothing else save sulphites, yeast and the opportunity to add enzymes and salt for the purposes of encouraging the keeving process. Today, a fabulous array of award-winning ciders are made right across the country, from the valleys in the south, to the mountains of Mid Wales, and all the way up to Anglesey.

Hallets Real Cider

Hafodyrynys, Newport

Standout cider: Original, 6% ABV

Style: Western Counties

Notes: It might sound silly, but this cider is really *cidery* on the nose. The phenolics are present but tempered, soft, and gently spicy. In the mouth the soft, clean elegance, creamy mid palate and savoury finish ensure this is a cider for everyone, whether they be a glugger or a sipper.

Hallets Cider is, according to Annie and Andy Hallett, the result of 'a hobby that got out of hand'. Situated on top of a hill on the eastern edge of the Welsh valleys, Hallets Cider is a byword for accessible yet complex tannin-forward ciders. You don't get too many smaller cider makers staring down a microscope to undertake a yeast count, but then not every cider maker was a successful engineer with an incredible attention to detail.

Palmers Upland Cyder

Rogertone, Newport

Standout cider: Little Jenny Wren, 6% ABV

Style: Western Counties

Notes: Phill must be a fan of puddings because tarte tatin and apple strudel leap out of the glass before you get anywhere near it. What a sensational colour, too – bold and brassy, just like its creator. The rich, bittersweet apple characters shine through – gentle clove spice and celeriac bitterness – while the golden syrup sweetness makes everything hum a little louder.

Phill Palmer, a Design and Technology School teacher, started making cyder in 2006 after falling in love with the straw-pressed cyder made at Haye Farm in Cornwall. Using his vocational skills, he built his own scratter and press and hasn't looked back since. He uses traditional cider apples and perry pears from unsprayed standard orchards, personally selecting, handling and washing every single apple that goes into his cider, before wild fermentation does its job. The results are an array of products, from still, to carbonated to keeved.

Monnow Valley Cider

Goytre, nr Usk

Standout cider: Frederick SV, 6% ABV

Style: Western Counties

Notes: Almost giving Foxwhelp a run for its money in the ultra-high electric acidity stakes, this cider is not for the faint-hearted, given there is no sweetness to ameliorate the zingy intensity. Fruity and fresh!

Having already lived in Monmouthsire for a number of years, it took a sip of cider at the Blorenge Bar at the Abergavenny Food festival for Kevin Garrod to be bitten by the bug. He soon found himself searching for apples and pear trees dotted around the landscape, often in beautiful old orchards. He went one step further and started making in 2015, with his cider and perries undergoing wild fermentation and no added sulphites. He particularly treasures the opportunity to pick at significant places, such as Perthyre farm at Rockfield, birthplace of the Breakwell's Seedling and Perthyre Cider apples, and where there are two very old Breakwell's Seedling trees still standing and just about bearing fruit.

Apple County Cider Co

Newcastle, Monmouthshire

Standout cider: Yarlington Mill SV, 5% ABV

Style: Western Counties

Notes: Gloriously deep amber hues entice you into this classic, award-winning cider. A remarkable minerality, which, in combination with the carbonation, creates a bridge to the back of the mouth which quickly gets washed away by a wave of juicy, bitter caramel loveliness.

Situated in the unspeakably beautiful border country between Monmouthshire and Herefordshire lies Whitehouse Farm and Apple County Cider. Using old bush orchards planted on the family farm in the 1960s, Ben Culpin has a number of classic varieties at his disposal, including Dabinett, Yarlington Mill and Brown's Apple, which generally end up as Single Varietal ciders. Ben uses a selected yeast strain to allow the nuances of the varieties to shine through in the fermentation, resulting in bold, intense tannic ciders.

Llanbethian Orchards

Cowbridge, Glamorgan

Standout cider: Katya Ice Cider, 8.4% ABV

Style: Ice

Notes: Showcasing a lot of skill, talent, time and cost, this is a wonderful cider. Lighter and fruitier than some ice ciders, but no less enjoyable, the sweetness is tempered by oak barrel toastiness, roast peaches, fresh citrus and elderflower.

While at University in Cardiff in the late 90s, Alex Simmens was involved in a real ale and cider society and ended up being the cider bar manager. Visits to the cider farms sparked a desire to have his own enterprise, culminating in him planting his own orchard in 2006. More so than many makers, Alex has exceedingly high standards. Nothing leaves the barn unless he is happy to drink it himself. He makes a range of different ciders and perries in different pack formats for different consumers and occasions – still draught in BIB and sparkling kegs for pubs, and 500ml and 750ml bottles for retail – but all wild fermented and 100% juice.

The Pembrokeshire Cider Co

Pembroke, Pembrokeshire

Standout cider: Henry VII, 6% ABV

Style: Western Counties

Notes: Smells like a vanilla sponge coming out of the oven, which is always a good place to start. Light, easy, accessible, and super fruity in the mid palate, this cider finishes with a slow, gentle, rising bitterness and astringency, but all delivered with a velveteen glove.

What happens when a publican, a hardware shop owner and a green-grocer look for a new hobby – a cidery, of course! Making 7,000 litres of cider in their first year and having planted 500 trees, Chris Scourfield (pints), David Halsted (paint) and Jon Ryan (parsnips) were looking to have some fun, earn a couple of quid and create a sustainable orchard environment. But winning a silver award with their very first product at the Welsh Perry & Cider Championships in 2018 spurred them on to grow the business even further, catering to the local and the tourist market through their Pembroke Castle themed brands.

Skyborry Cider & Perry

Knighton, Powys

Standout cider: Pommage, 5% ABV

Style: Keeved

Notes: The essence of keeved cider. Sweet leather, tobacco and sweet tarriness combine with prickly acidity and a tug of grippy astringency. Glorious.

Brothers Dani and Adam Davies work with local orchard owners, and by placing an emphasis on select, high quality fruit, Skyborry ciders are characterised by their minimal intervention nature. The majority of their range is bottle conditioned, often with some level of natural carbonation and often with some residual sweetness from unfermented sugars. Fermentations are slowed by racking during cold snaps in the winter, which they describe as an intuitive but imprecise method, ending up with ciders and perries on a spectrum of both sweetness and carbonation.

Jaspels Fine Cider Makers

Aberffraw, Isle of Anglesey

Standout cider: Woodland, 6% ABV

Style: Western Counties x Eastern Counties

Notes: Smooth! Wonderful cinnamon, vanilla and butterscotch shines through, but has lovely brisk acidity and lush, mouth-filling soft tannins ensuring it doesn't become too flabby. A gorgeous apple pie in a bottle.

Ade Percival had made ciders and wines as a hobby since his mid-20s for his personal use, but it wasn't until his late 40s, after he and wife Janet relocated to the Isle of Anglesey, that the idea of making cider on a larger scale took hold. Using a blend of locally sourced dessert apples and tannic apples grown further south, they can create a range of flavour profiles. Not satisfied with simply making a 'dry' and 'sweet', Ade and Janet are constantly experimenting, whether it be ciders that are traditionally still, Pét Nat ciders or fruit flavoured, while they are releasing their first traditional bottle-fermented cider, Môn Katja, in 2021.

Welsh Mountain Cider

Llanidloes, Powys

Standout cider: Somerset Redstreak SV, 5.8% ABV

Style: Western Counties

Notes: Intense savoury aromas lead onto a cider with great taste and mouthfeel complexity. MLF brings creaminess, minerality shows up to the party and an almost Riesling-like fusol note lingers. Lightly grippy, heavily complex.

Chava Richman comes from wine country in California and has always been interested in apples and orchards. Her original plan was to come to the UK to learn more about cider and take back her knowledge and a few varieties. Instead, she fell in love with cider, and a cider maker, and was lucky enough to join Bill Bleasdale on his 6-acre smallholding in the wilds of Mid Wales to plant apples, grow trees and build up what is now Welsh Mountain Cider. Together they make natural, live ciders from 100% freshly pressed fruit, fermented using wild yeasts without the use of sulphur or stabilisation. They grow a remarkable 450 varieties of apple, enabling them to make ciders ranging from light and crisp dessert fruit blends through to rich and tannic bittersweet styles. They are then cellar aged for anywhere between six months and six years, continuing to mature in the bottle.

Scotland

The most northerly part of Britain certainly produces its fair share of alcoholic drinks, but it would be fair to say that cider is not one of its more heralded libations. To an extent this is a product of pure geography – large swathes of Scotland are simply too cold and/or wet to efficiently grow fruit. There are some meso-climates which historically supported orchards, and still do today, such as the Clyde Valley and the Carse of Gowrie in Perthshire, although their numbers have reduced dramatically since the 1950s, with a recent survey identifying only 880 Scottish orchards.

Despite this heritage, there doesn't appear to be any evidence of cider making taking place in Scotland historically, with the theory being that the apples were considered more valuable as a food than as drink. Rather wonderfully, that's all starting to change. Pioneering Scottish producer Ryan Sealey, proprietor of the Caledonian Cider Company (from whom much of this Scottish insight derives) considers there to be a distinctly aspirational thread to Scottish cider makers, owing to not being shackled to any heritage or culture. The majority of inspiration comes from English cider making, it would seem, but with plenty of experimentation and playfulness, whether it be using specialised techniques such as keeving and bottle fermenting, as well as the use of locally sourced whisky barrels for maturation.

Novar Cider

Dingwall, Highlands

Standout cider: Novar 2019, 5% ABV

Style: Eastern Counties x Western Counties

Notes: Beautiful herbaceous aromas swill around the glass enticing you to dive in.
On the palate, the light, lean acidity gently cuts through a touch of sweetness,
allowing gentle creaminess and super smooth tannins to hug the tongue.

William Munro Ferguson heralds from the Novar Estate, just north
of Inverness – not your typical cider country. But such was his
passion for cider that he sought out a mentor, who turned out to be
Eric Borderelt in Normandy, one of the world's most revered makers.
Wishing to make cider that emulated the tannic qualities he loved,
he selected 21 classic West Country varieties, plus a few heritage
Highland varieties, and planted 3,000 trees overlooking the Firth
of Cromarty. William macerates the pulp and allows a long, slow,
wild fermentation, bringing great depth to his cider.

The Wee Scottish Cider Co

Aberdeen

Standout cider: Seidear, 7% ABV

Style: Keeved x Bottle-Fermented

Notes: Clean as a whistle, zingy, crisp and fresh, but with a gorgeous,
soft, buttery croissant edge. Delicious.

The name of Christian Stolte's cider enterprise is accurately small,
but he is already selling more than he can make in the garage underneath his house on the outskirts of Aberdeen. The fruit is sourced
from the walled gardens of local estates, before being keeved and then
undergoing a bottle fermentation. To those who pooh-pooh the idea
that Scotland can produce great ciders, his riposte is, 'The great wines
of the world are matured in caves at temperatures around 10°C and in
Scotland we are blessed with this temperature all year around!'

Cairn o' Mohr Fruit Wine and Cider

Errol, Perth & Kinross

Standout cider: King Jimmy's Cider, 5% ABV

Style: Eastern Counties

Notes: Never before has a cider smelt and tasted more like a Margarita cocktail. Intense heathery, salty and citrus aromas flow out of the glass before bursting to life with the most beautifully vibrant quince intensity. Amazing!

Situated in the Carse of Gowrie, one of the most famed apple, plum and raspberry growing areas in Scotland, Ron and Judith Gillies established Cairn o' Mohr Winery in 1987 to explore the fermentative opportunities these local fruits can provide. Like ancient monuments, remnants of the old orchards still exist, dotted around the Carse, which Ron and Judith use along with the fruit from a number of modern orchards in the local area.

Steilhead Cider

Nithsdale, Dumfriesshire

Standout cider: Bullfinch Dry, 6% ABV

Style: Western Counties

Notes: Gentle, smoky phenolics give an indication of the tannic behemoth that sits underneath, but a wonderfully calm and balanced one at that, with a zip of acidity, punchy fruitiness and a giant smooth hug from the barrel.

Being the son of a cider and perry-making legend was always going to be an advantage when it came to learning the dark arts of its making for Max Nowell and wife, Penny. Trying to undertake that making closer to Kirkwall than King's Caple, wasn't. But their wonderful orchard full of bittersweet and bittersharp apples are proof that it can be done, and ruddy well too. Variously mixing these tannic apples with a few sourced from Herefordshire and local sharp apples enables Max and Penny to make a range of bone dry, wild fermented ciders that Jean Nowell would rightly be proud of.

Ireland

Ireland has an ancient apple and orchard heritage – equal to anything in North-West Europe. According to Mark Jenkinson, writing on behalf of Cider Ireland, 'Thanks to the work of the late Dr J. G. Lamb and more recently the Irish Seedsavers Association, the Armagh Orchards Trust and University College Dublin, over 70 distinctly Irish varieties of apple trees have now been identified and documented from all over Ireland.' He continues, 'The earliest mention of specifically Irish varieties of apple trees occurs in 1598 when a writer discusses the fruitful nature of Irish orchards and the merits of the fine old Irish varieties contained in them.'

The zenith of Irish apple growing was reached in the 19th century, with varieties being exported to England. Today, the predominant apple variety grown in Ireland is Bramley, the name of which has protected status in Armagh. Originally grown for culinary purposes, it provides a high acid cider that must be treated with care. Around the Emerald Isle, but especially in Armagh, Antrim, Meath, Cavan, Cork, Tipperary and Waterford, there are decent tracts of dessert apples grown, and even the odd pocket of bittersweet apples, too, providing a broad range of styles.

Stonewell Cider

Kinsale, County Cork

Standout cider: Tawny, 15% ABV

Style: Hopped Apple Wine

Notes: Under the sub-brand Nohoval comes a drink that I'm not really sure how to describe. Made through mega chaptalisation, but with arrestation before all the sugar has fermented, and then dry hopped. The impression is more of a dry port – deep, rich, warm, glowing, unexpected, gorgeous.

Irish craft cider pioneer, and Chair of Cider Ireland, Daniel Emerson is on a mission to change consumer's perceptions about Irish cider. He is doing so by making a range of ciders that put the apple front and centre, and sometimes the odd other ingredient, too (the rhubarb is a winner). Daniel works with growers in Laois, Tipperary and Cork to supply dessert, culinary and tannic apples, helping to achieve this range of products.

Longueville House Cider

Mallow, County Cork

Standout cider: Mor, 8% ABV

Style: Western Counties

Notes: Big, intense, savoury, almost meaty phenolics leap from the glass upon pouring, and the intensity doesn't stop when it gets into your mouth. Boosted by a dash of cider spirit, everything is dialled up to 11 here – oily sweetness, umami brothy bitterness, balsamic sourness and roasted fire pit warmth to finish things off.

Michael Callaghan was a bit of a visionary, planting Cork's first vineyard back in the 1970s. The Irish weather got the better of the vines and Michael used to joke that he was waiting for global warming and for the great Champagne houses of France to buy land in England (he was obviously a soothsayer). It was then that he turned his attention to apples, planting Michelin and Dabinett for making cider and apple brandy. He became the first person in Ireland, outside the big three established national distillers, to get a licence and so became the first person since the 1770s to reintroduce to Ireland the practice of distilling cider. Today, son William is at the helm of the enterprise, overseeing the making of the wild ferment ciders and resultant spirits.

Longmeadow Cider

Portadown, County Armagh

Standout cider: Medium, 4.5% ABV

Style: Eastern Counties

Notes: Citrus and peaches shine through in this zingy, crisp, bold and remarkably intense cider, especially considering its relatively low alcohol content.

Based in the Apple County of Armagh, it's a real family affair at Longmeadow cider, with husband and wife Pat and Catherine McKeever joined in the business by son Peter. Together they seek to make the best of Irish cider 'from plant to pour'. The majority of fruit is hand-picked on the family farm just outside Portadown, where a wide range of dessert and Bramley apples are grown. The ciders are allowed to ferment naturally before achieving a reduction of the alcohol and an introduction of sweetness in the final product through adding apple back to the cider.

Tempted Cider

Lisburn, County Antrim

Standout cider: Dry, 5.7% ABV

Style: Western Counties x Eastern Counties

Notes: This is a really clever cider, managing to be at once quite impressively layered and complex, and yet also immensely, easily drinkable at the same time. A salty and gently smoky nose entices further investigation, and clean citrus, raspberry liquorice and soft tannins are what can be found.

Tempted is the result of an entrepreneurial apple-growing family trying to add value to their crop as demand for dessert and culinary apples decreases. Having fond memories of making fruit wine with his father, Davy Uprichard turned his hand to cider making as a hobby, with decent results, and so, in 2013, Tempted was born. It's a real family affair, with wife, Janet, and daughters, Sara and Jenni, all involved. Davy is a real tinkerman, sourcing differing varieties, playing with additional flavours and also undertaking ageing.

Cider Terms

Acetic acid The most common cider fault, it is the result of the conversion of alcohol to acetic acid (vinegar) achieved via acetic acid bacteria in the presence of oxygen. The desired concentration of acetic characteristics is subjective, but when it entirely dominates, the appreciation of cider diminishes.

Acid One of the primary components of smell, taste and mouthfeel in an apple and resultant cider. It is characterised by crisp, zingy, fresh and cutting sensations. The primary, natural acid in apples is malic acid, whereas pears contain malic acid and citric Acid.

Acidity The level of acid within an apple and cider.

Aromatic A cider exuding intense, fresh, fruity, herbaceous, perfumed smells, generally caused by a natural compound called esters found within certain apples.

Astringent A mouthfeel sensation of mouth drying and puckering resulting from the presence of tannins. Can range from soft and gentle furriness to full face-distorting grippiness.

Balance The interplay and harmonisation of various sensations, primarily between acid, tannin, sweetness and mouthfeel.

Barnyard A coverall term describing certain aromas and taste impressions of ciders made from tannic apples. Can range from light, fresh, herbaceous 'hay barn' to rich and organic to faecal.

Bitterness A taste sensation provided by tannins. These can range from gentle spiciness to harsh woodiness.

Bittersharp An apple which contains higher levels of acidity and tannin.

Bittersweet An apple which contains higher levels of both tannin *and* acidity.

Body A perception of how much the cider fills the mouth.

Bottle-Conditioned (1) A naturally sparkling cider achieved through a minor secondary in-bottle fermentation, without disgorging.

Bottle-Conditioned (2) Or a naturally sparkling cider achieved through finishing its *primary* fermentation in the bottle, rather than a *secondary*. The cider is moved from the vessel to the bottle while there is still sugar to be fermented. Depending on how the fermentation has been managed and the intention of the cider maker, the cider may complete fermentation and end up bone dry (known as Pét Nat in natural wine circles, and increasingly with some cider makers) or retain some residual sweetness via an initial process of cold racking or keeving.

Bottle-Fermented (see p.163).

Brettanomyces (see Phenolic) A naturally occurring yeast which precipitates the creation of phenolic compounds, common to Western Counties and Keeved ciders. The desired concentration of *Bretty* characteristics is subjective, but when it entirely dominates, the appreciation of cider diminishes and would be considered a fault.

Carbonation The level of sparkle within a cider, whether derived naturally or through force carbonation, ranging from still to petillant to medium to high.

Charmat method A naturally sparkling cider achieved through undertaking the final portion of fermentation in a pressure tank prior to bottling, frequently with residual sugar leftover. This is the process used to make Prosecco wine.

Chewy A term that describes the mouthfeel of tannic ciders with great mouthfeel.

Clarity An assessment of how clear the cider is, ranging from cloudy to hazy to clear.

Clear A cider with high levels of transparency, normally as a result of being filtered.

Cloudy A cider with a high degree of opacity.

Complex A cider with many different, concurrent aroma, taste and mouthfeel sensations.

Crisp (see Acid)

Cut (see Acid) The action of acidity reducing the perception of sweetness.

Dry The total, or perceived lack of, sweetness in a cider. Perception of dryness can be increased with ciders containing tannin.

Earthy Aroma and taste sensation associated with ciders with tannin.

Esters Compounds derived from certain apples providing fruity, oil, fresh, herbaceous, perfumed and confected aromas.

Ethyl acetate An ester produced naturally by certain, generally non-Saccharomyces, yeasts in the presence of oxygen. Their presence is detected by a smell
and taste reminiscent of nail varnish remover. The desired concentration
of solventy characteristics is subjective, but when it entirely dominates,
the appreciation of cider diminishes and would be considered a fault.

Filtered The process of removing any particulates in the cider to make it clear.

Finish The sensation associated with the length of time one can taste, smell and
feel a cider past the point of tasting.

Floral The perfumed, aromatic sensation of flowers and blossom.

Fruity The presence of aromas and tastes that exude characters from fruits
including apple and pear, as well as citrus fruits, stone fruits and tropical
fruits.

Hazy A cider without full, bright clarity, but not full opacity.

Herbaceous Aroma and taste sensation ranging from gentle woodiness to
herbs to vegetal.

Integration The level at which of various sensations, primarily acid, tannin and
sweetness, meld together to form a continuous flavour profile.

Intensity The perception of how bold or strong any particular aroma or taste
is within a cider.

Keeved (see p.154).

Lactic An aroma and taste sensation derived from MLF, providing elements
of butterscotch, creaminess and yoghurt.

Medicinal Aroma and taste sensation reminiscent of antiseptic ointment.
Associated with ciders made from tannic apples.

Malolactic Fermentation (MLF) A spontaneous, non-alcoholic fermentation of
naturally occurring malic acid into lactic acid by lactic acid bacteria (LAB).

Mouse A fault whose presence is thought to result from the actions of certain
lactic acid bacteria or possibly *Brettanomyces*. Its presence cannot be detected
on the aroma, but provides a growing musty, fusty, acrid 'mouse cage' taste
at the back of the throat. Individual sensitivity varies from person to person,
but it is widely agreed to be a fault with no desired concentrations.

Mouthfeel The perceived level of body texture in the mouth, influenced by
tannin, acidity, sweetness, carbonation, alcohol level.

Oxidised A cider that has had a prolonged exposure to oxygen, creating a
darkening of colouration and a reduction of acidity and fruitiness.
Often reminiscent of sherry-like characters, the desired concentration
of oxidised characteristics is subjective, but when it entirely dominates,
the appreciation of cider diminishes and it would be considered a fault.

Pét Nat (see Bottle-Conditioned 2).

Phenolic Overarching name for the aroma compounds derived from tannic apples, including medicinal, woody, spicy, earthy and barnyard.

Savoury (aka umami) One of the five basic tastes, this provides 'meaty' characters found within soy sauce, mushrooms and Parmesan cheese and is common in cider with higher levels of tannin.

Sharp (apple) An apple that contains higher levels of acidity and lower levels of tannin.

Sharp (sensation, see Acid).

Solventy (see Ethyl acetate).

Spicy The presence of aromas and flavours reminiscent of clove, nutmeg, cinnamon, etc.

Structure (see Complex).

Sulphides A fault caused by stressed yeast, precipitating highly concentrated aromas, and to a lesser extent, tastes. Hydrogen Sulphide is reminiscent of ammonia and rotten eggs, while the more complex disulphides are redolent of rotten cabbages and dirty drains. This is widely agreed to be a fault with no desired concentrations.

Sulphites Sulphur dioxide, used in the cider making process as an anti-microbial and preservative agent.

Sweet (apple) An apple that contains lower levels of both acidity *and* tannin.

Sweet (sensation) The actual, or perceived, presence of a high level of sugar, or sweetener, in a cider. Perception of sweetness can be increased with ciders that have undergone MLF.

Terroir (see p.173) The combined environmental factors that impact upon the characteristics and properties of a crop (in this case apples and pears), incorporating: climate, soil type, underlying geology, topography and aspect.

Texture (see Mouthfeel).

Thin The perception of a cider lacking intensity, body and mouthfeel.

Tannin Compound found in apples classically grown in the western counties of England and Welsh Borders, and now grown all over Britain. Contributes towards mouthfeel (astringent) and taste (bitter, woody, earthy, savoury, medicinal, spicy) sensations.

Umami (see Savoury).

Vintage (see p.175) The cider made from any given year, and potentially the sensorial differences between them owing to the human or natural variations year on year.

Woody The aroma and taste sensation, real or perceived, or characters reminiscent of wood or wooden casks.

Zingy (see Acid).

References

Books

BROWN, P., *Craft: An Argument*, 2020, Storm Lantern Books

BRUNING, T., *Golden Fire: The Story of Cider*, 2012,
Authors Online Ltd.

CHARLEY, V.L.S., The Principles and Practice of
Cider Making, (A Translation of *La Cidrerie* by
G. Warcollier 1928), 1949, Leonard Hill.

FRENCH, R.K., *The History and Virtues of Cyder*, 1982,
Robert Hale Ltd.

JEFFRYS, H. *Empire of Booze*, 2018, Penguin.

STONE, A., *In Search of Cider*, 2012. somersethistory.co.uk

WILKINSON, L.P., *Bulmers of Hereford: A Century of
Cider Making*, 1987, Henry & Charles.

Reports and papers

CABRAS, I., & HIGGINS, D.M., 'Beer, brewing, and business
history', *Business History*, 2016, 58:5, pp. 609–624.

Defra Statistics: Agricultural Facts England Regional
Profiles, March 2021

DURHAM, Herbert E., 'Perry Pear Trees and Perry',
Woolhope Naturalist's Field Club Papers, 1923.

GOUGH, J.B., 'Winecraft and Chemistry in 18th-Century
France: Chaptal and the Invention of Chaptalization',
Technology and Culture, vol. 39, no. 1, 1998, pp. 74–104.

LEA, A., *An Assessment of Chemical Markers for
The Establishment of Juice Content In Ciders.*
Food Standards Agency, 2004. Accessed via
www.cider.org.uk/juice_content_in_ciders.pdf

LLOYD, Amy J., 'Education, Literacy and the Reading
Public', (British Library Newspapers, Detroit: Gale, 2007).

Mintel Beer Market Report, 2020

THOMPSON, O., *Notes Towards a History of Norfolk Cider*, 2017.
Downloaded via www.cideruk.org

Westons Cider Report (WCR) 2018, 2019, 2020,
2020 Covid-19 Update, 2021

Wine GB Annual Report 2020

Websites

www.legislation.gov.uk/uksro/1932/705/pdfs/
uksro_19320705_en.pdf

www.gov.uk/government/publications/
excise-notice-162-cider-production/
excise-notice-162-cider-production

www.morningadvertiser.co.uk/Article/2019/12/09/
What-s-the-UK-s-best-selling-cider

www.theguardian.com/lifeandstyle/2011/apr/17/
cider-industry-protected-expense-alcoholics

www.thegrocer.co.uk/pear-cider-ruling-gives-
perry-a-timely-boost-/119462.article

www.fao.org/fao-who-codexalimentarius/
about-codex/en/

www.cideruk.com/apple-growers

www.goodbeerhunting.com/blog/2017/8/28/statue-
worthy-remembering-michael-jacksons-impact-
on-belgian-beer-10-years-after-his-death

www.devoncidermakersguild.com

www.worcestershireorchards.co.uk

www.bramleyapples.co.uk

www.thornboroughcider.co.uk/yorkshire-cider

www.orchardrevival.org.uk

www.ciderireland.com

www.thedrinksbusiness.com/2019/01/researchers-
uncover-73-new-welsh-apple-and-pear-varieties

CAMRA Books

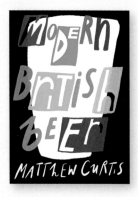

Modern British Beer
MATTHEW CURTIS

This book is about why modern British beer is important. Over the course of the past two decades the British beer scene as we know it has changed, forever. Matthew Curtis gives a personal insight into the eclectic and exciting world of modern British beer from a choice of 86 influential brews; from how they taste, how their ingredients are sourced, to the engaging stories of the people behind the scenes working hard to bring exciting beer to drinkers all over Britain. This book is a fantastic starting point to explore British beer with an exciting location closer than you think.

RRP £15.99   ISBN 978-1-85249-370-7

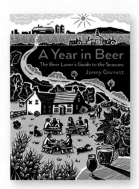

A Year in Beer
JONNY GARRETT

Chefs have been telling us to eat seasonally for decades, yet, when it comes to drink, we tend to reach for the same thing, whatever time of year. But beer is inextricably linked to the seasons, and thinking about it all seasonally opens the door to even greater beer experiences. *A Year in Beer* is an exploration of how our ingredients and tastes change with the seasons, and how Britain's rich brewing history still influences us today. Discover the best UK beer experiences, from summer beer festivals to the autumn hop and apple harvests – taking in the glory of the seasons that make them all possible.

RRP £15.99   ISBN 978-1-85249-372-1

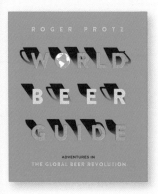

World Beer Guide
ROGER PROTZ

The world of beer is on fire. Traditional brewing countries are witnessing a spectacular growth in the number of beer makers while drinkers in such unlikely nations as France and Italy are moving from the grape to the grain. Drawing on decades of experience, Roger Protz takes readers on a journey of discovery around the world's favourite alcoholic drink – uncovering the interlinked stories behind the best breweries and beers across every continent in the world.

RRP £30   ISBN 978-1-85249-373-8

Order these and other CAMRA Books from **shop.camra.org.uk**

Thank you to all of the
following who pledged support
for this publication

ALEXANDER J. AL   ROBIN BORNOFF   AMBROSIA BOROWSKI

MICHAEL CAINE   BRIAN CAMERON, FORT WORTH, TEXAS

CANTERBURY CIDER THE MAYLAM FAMILY   AL COLLAR   PETE ELDERTON

MARK GARNER   ROBERT HANDEBO   STUART HASSAL   GRANT HUTCHISON (re:stalk ltd)

LUKE KEATLEY-CLARKE   GED KILKENNY   ROBERT KING   TONY LEA

THE LICENSING GUYS   IAIN R LOE   MANCHESTER CIDER CLUB   KEV MATTHEWS

JULES MERCER   CATERINA MOLINARI   COLIN NICHOLSON

TOM OLIVER (Oliver's Cider & Perry)   MARKUS RAUPACH, BAMBERG

DARREN SALLIS   DAVID SAX   JANE STEVENSON   CHRIS STRINGER

ALISON TAFFS   MICHAEL TREACHER   JIM WAKEFIELD

MELINDA J. WAKEFIELD   MICHAEL AND FIONA WHEELER

ANDY WILLIS, SOMERSET